LATE STEVENS

B. J. LEGGETT

LATE STEVENS
The Final Fiction

LOUISIANA STATE UNIVERSITY PRESS   BATON ROUGE

First printing

DESIGNER: AMANDA MCDONALD SCALLAN
TYPEFACE: MINION
TYPESETTER: G&S TYPESETTERS
PRINTER AND BINDER: THOMSON-SHORE, INC.

Library of Congress Cataloging-in-Publication Data

Leggett, B. J. (Bobby Joe), 1938–
    Late Stevens : the final fiction / B. J. Leggett.
        p. cm.
    Includes bibliographical references and index.
    ISBN 0-8071-3057-5 (cloth : alk. paper)
    1. Stevens, Wallace, 1879–1955—Criticism and interpretation. I. Title.
PS3537.T4753Z67435 2005
811'.52—DC22

                                                            2004022077

For Corinne

CONTENTS

PREFACE ix

ABBREVIATIONS xiii

1 / Stevens' Final Fiction 1

2 / Schopenhauer and the Two Worlds of *The Rock* 22

3 / Penelope, Mr. Homburg, and the Interior Paramour 47

4 / At the Convent of the Blue Nuns: "To an Old
    Philosopher in Rome" 73

5 / Reconstructing "The Rock": Stevens and Misreading 93

6 / Conclusion: After the *Collected Poems* 113

NOTES 145

BIBLIOGRAPHY 157

INDEX 163

In the course of reading Wallace Stevens' last poems I may appear at times to be characterizing all previous criticism as wrongheaded and my own as a necessary corrective. While that is not precisely my claim, I must acknowledge disputing an unusually large number of readings of the late poems in the six chapters that follow. And because it is necessary to specify the manner in which these poems have been read, I incorporate an unusually wide range of earlier commentary. As is the practice of most interpretative studies, I am indeed attempting to contest earlier readings and replace them with my own. What I do not claim is that mine is the definitive reading that will put an end to debate on late Stevens. I don't know, first of all, how we would recognize a definitive reading if we came across it, and the commentary on Stevens' late poems is no less perceptive and intelligent than the commentary on earlier volumes. Furthermore, the late poems appear to contain fewer real difficulties for the reader. After the opacity and abstraction of Stevens' three preceding volumes (*Parts of a World, Transport to Summer,* and *The Auroras of Autumn*), the poems of the final section of the *Collected Poems,* titled *The Rock,* and the uncollected poems published in *Opus Posthumous,* the two groups I designate as late Stevens, are refreshingly personal and accessible, with a few notable exceptions. Most of these exceptions are found among the uncollected poems—very late Stevens. Yet two of the best-known poems from *The Rock*—"To an Old Philosopher in Rome" and the title poem—have resisted easy access, and I have devoted some attention to the issues they raise.

One of the issues raised by *The Rock*'s title poem is in fact that of misreading, both as the term is understood in poststructuralist criticism and as it is understood in a more traditional sense, what deconstruction sometimes labels "weak" misreading, an erroneous reading that may be corrected. As an exercise in reading a significant body of Stevens' poetry, this study cannot escape the issue of misreading in both senses. The two readers who figure most prominently here, J. Hillis Miller and Harold Bloom, have perhaps been the chief popularizers of the concept of misreading, and I am indebted to both. Miller's influential reading of "The Rock" not only shaped the poem for subsequent readers but helped to introduce deconstructive criticism to the American academy. To challenge his reading may appear foolhardy, since the rhetoric of deconstruction is notoriously difficult to assail, but I have attempted to show how he "weakly" misreads the poem. Bloom has been perhaps more responsible than any other critic for Stevens' high place in twentieth-century poetry, and I agree with his overall judgment of the late poems, as well as his conclusion that "Stevens' last phase . . . was his best."[1] I have, however, disputed his reading of some of these poems, particularly his interpretation of one key poem of *The Rock*, "Final Soliloquy of the Interior Paramour," which, I believe, mistakes both the identity of the "Interior Paramour" of the title and the nature of the speaker of the poem. What I have tried to show is that the significance of poems such as "The Rock" and "Final Soliloquy of the Interior Paramour" (as opposed simply to their meaning) may be more clearly read in relation to the themes, motifs, and, particularly, the fictions that underlie the late poems as a whole.

The distinction between significance and meaning is one I have borrowed from Michael Riffaterre, although I may not always be faithful to his own use of the terms. In *Semiotics of Poetry*, Riffaterre characterizes meaning as the contextual understanding of a work, the understanding dictated by the work's grammar and syntax. Significance, however, is the consequence of a second stage of reading, an intertextual reading that goes beyond grammar to explain what Riffaterre calls "ungrammatical" features of the text, not violations of grammar but passages that cannot be adequately read simply by means of the grammar. The significance of a text may be incompatible with its contextual or grammatical meaning, referring the reader instead to an intertext or set of intertexts. For Riffaterre, intertexts are cultural or literary texts, conventions, descriptive systems, clichés, or commonplaces the text has absorbed.[2] I have identified a number of intertexts which the late poems have incorporated, including texts from Arthur Schopenhauer and George Santayana (Nietzsche, who inhabited the early poems, seems notably absent from late Stevens), but by far the most pervasive intertext of the late poems is one of Stevens' own fictions, on which so much of the late poetry rests. The failure to recognize the presence of this fiction in a particular poem—say, "The Rock" or "Final Soliloquy of the Interior Paramour"—does not inevitably result in a misreading in Miller's or Bloom's sense or even in a traditional sense, but rather in an inadequate or incomplete reading of Stevens. Charles Berger's Bloom-influenced *Forms of Farewell: The Late Poetry of Wallace Stevens*, for example, is certainly not wrongheaded in its discussion of the last decade of Stevens' poetry, but for a study that looks at the "guiding . . . obsessions"[3] that characterize this period, it reveals a curious neglect of a concept with which Stevens was then preoccupied. *Late Stevens* is an endeavor to disclose what has obviously been difficult to read in the last poems. Stevens' final fiction is not the whole story of these poems, but a reading of them, I want to show, is incomplete without it.

I wish to thank the *Wallace Stevens Journal* for permission to reprint, with slight alterations, material that comprises chapter 5 and a portion of chapter 3. Quotations from Stevens' poetry are from the *Collected Poems of Wallace Stevens* and *Opus Posthumous*, published by Alfred A. Knopf.

ABBREVIATIONS

Counsels	Arthur Schopenhauer. *Counsels and Maxims: Being the Second Part of Arthur Schopenhauer's Aphorismen zur Lebensweisheit.* Trans. T. Bailey Saunders. London, 1924.
CP	Wallace Stevens. *The Collected Poems of Wallace Stevens.* New York, 1954.
IPR	George Santayana. *Interpretations of Poetry and Religion.* Ed. William G. Holzberger and Herman J. Saatkamp Jr. Cambridge, Mass., 1989.
Letters	Wallace Stevens. *Letters of Wallace Stevens.* Ed. Holly Stevens. New York, 1977.
NA	Wallace Stevens. *The Necessary Angel: Essays on Reality and the Imagination.* New York, 1951.
OP	Wallace Stevens. *Opus Posthumous.* Ed. Milton J. Bates. New York, 1989.
Persons	George Santayana. *Persons and Places.* 3 vols. New York, 1944–1953.
Philosophy	George Santayana. *The Philosophy of George Santayana.* Ed. Paul Arthur Schilpp. Evanston, 1940.
Wisdom	Arthur Schopenhauer. *The Wisdom of Life: Being the First Part of Arthur Schopenhauer's Aphorismen zur Lebensweisheit.* Trans. T. Bailey Saunders. London, 1924.
World	Arthur Schopenhauer. *The World as Will and Idea.* 3 vols. Trans. R. B. Haldane and J. Kemp. London, 1883.

1 / Stevens' Final Fiction

The exquisite truth is to know that it is a fiction and that you believe in it willingly.
— STEVENS, "Adagia," *Opus Posthumous*

WHEN, IN THE YEAR before his death, Wallace Stevens was asked to supply a statement of the major ideas in his work, his response was in one regard surprising. A reader who had followed his career to that point might have anticipated an account centered on what he termed his "imagination-reality complex" (*Letters* 792), since his collection of theoretical papers, *The Necessary Angel,* published three years earlier, had been subtitled *Essays on Reality and the Imagination.* Yet in the statement written to accompany the reprinting of "The Auroras of Autumn" Stevens marginalizes the imagination-reality theme in deference to another concept he now regards as more central: "There are many poems relating to the interactions between reality and imagination, which are to be regarded as marginal to this central theme," which is "the possibility of a supreme fiction, recognized as a fiction, in which men could propose to themselves a fulfilment" (*Letters* 820).

Stevens is careful not to say that his work embodies such a fiction, only that it suggests the possibility of one. As in his most ambitious treatment of the concept, "Notes toward a Supreme Fiction," his construction here appears to place it in the future, although the phrasing is ambiguous: "In the creation of any such fiction, poetry would have a vital significance" (*Letters* 820). More than a decade earlier, after the publication of "Notes," Stevens had made a number of similarly guarded statements with the same implications. "I have no idea of the form that a supreme fiction would take," he had told Henry Church, to whom the poem was dedicated (*Letters* 430); he also had told Hi Simons that "Notes" had not in fact adequately characterized the supreme fiction: "I ought to say that I have not defined a supreme fiction. . . . In principle there appear to be certain characteristics of a supreme fiction *and the Notes is confined to a statement of a few of those characteristics*" (*Letters* 435; Stevens' underlining).

The supreme fiction is an old and complicated story in Stevens criticism that, as he noted, "could occupy a school of rabbis for the next few generations" (*Letters* 435), and I don't intend to reopen the whole issue. I want to pursue initially a collateral issue, which can be stated as a set of questions. Does Stevens' 1954 statement, in which the possible supreme fiction has become the "central theme" of his work, reflect a change in his thinking about the concept from the earlier "Notes"? Is the statement related to the poetry Stevens was writing in the last years of his life, that is, primarily the poems that became *The Rock,* the final section of the *Collected Poems*? Does Stevens' poetry embody or realize a version of the supreme fiction or does his work merely suggest some of the characteristics such an unrealizable concept might take?

It is this last option that Stevens' critics have generally chosen, following the drift of what appears to be his own view. William York Tindall calls "Notes toward a Supreme Fiction" "a preliminary draft of the great poem [Stevens] will never write." Joseph Riddel concludes that "Stevens' search for the ultimate or central or supreme speaks always in terms of possibility, of the potential of the mind and not of actuality." Robert Rehder notes that the supreme fiction "is something that 'is going to be.'" For Daniel Schwarz, it "exists always as possibility, as ideal," and for Rafeev Patke, "Notes" "concedes not a necessary arrival but only the recession of a theoretical possibility, always toward, toward, but never finally there."[1]

The most recent version of the view that the poetry can only gesture *toward* the supreme fiction, never arriving at it, is articulated in David Jarraway's study of the question of belief in Stevens. Jarraway rechristens the supreme fiction the "Supreme Absence" and writes, "It would become the fiction (or the abstract) that one approached asymptotically, so to speak, the 'Limitless' for which the more one compiled one's 'notes,' the more one sensed its retreat further away into the abyss of distance." "Notes toward a Supreme Fiction" is "a discourse directed toward metaphysical absence" that turns the question of belief into "an infinitely renewable problematic." To read the later poems in the light of "Notes," he finds, is to see them as "a discontinuous series of attempts or random wagers at moments more or less fraught with spiritual insight . . . without the expectation of some kind of apodictic payoff lying in store at the close of a seamless, epiphanic theodicy or of any other such conventionally homogeneous master narrative."[2]

I want to suggest that there *is* a kind of master narrative in Stevens' last poems, especially those that comprise *The Rock*—or more properly, perhaps, a master intertext, since it is not always explicitly present in the poems—and that this intertext is based on the supreme fiction. I want to argue that Stevens' concept of the supreme fiction has mutated by the time of his last poems, since he comes more and more to give form to what was formless in "Notes," and that his 1954 statement is colored by the fact that the supreme fiction has become the central preoccupation of the poetry he is writing at the time. My argument, in other words, is that Stevens' late poetry, unlike "Notes," does in fact embody a version of the supreme fiction, not merely as description or illustration but as a belief given concrete form, realized.

I am not the first of Stevens' readers to interpret his late poems in the context of the supreme fiction. In a recent study, Janet McCann notes correctly that Stevens' "late poems show an attempt to represent the supreme fiction as something beyond poetry, something to which poetry is an approach." She points to the "transcendent vision" of the last poems and places great significance on Stevens' apparent deathbed conversion, which she calls "a final leap of faith" that adds the "never-written fourth criterion for his supreme fiction: 'It must be human.'"[3]

Joseph Carroll's excellent *Wallace Stevens' Supreme Fiction* makes the most extensive and detailed argument for the presence of the supreme fiction in the later poems. Against the grain of Stevens criticism, Carroll argues that Stevens finally arrives at his supreme fiction in three late poems, "The Owl in the Sarcophagus," "The Auroras of Autumn," and "A Primitive Like an Orb." In these poems Stevens "gathers together the ideas and images of a poetic lifetime, and he fashions these materials into a comprehensive mythology of life, death, and the imagination." After the visionary poems of *The Auroras of Autumn* Carroll finds, however, that Stevens enters a new phase of experience, a confrontation with "the poverty of old age," which carries with it a decline of visionary power. With the exception of a few poems in *The Rock,* such as the title poem, "Final Soliloquy of the Interior Paramour," and "To an Old Philosopher in Rome," "he can no longer look forward to a culminating moment of visionary realization," and "he redefines the visionary goal as an ever-receding ideal." According to Carroll, "The Plain Sense of Things" reveals that "Stevens' 'fantastic effort' to create a supreme fiction has failed to fix itself in a permanent realization," and "The Rock" gives evidence "that Stevens' visionary power 'is exhausted and a little old.'"[4]

Although Carroll's reading of the three visionary poems of *The Auroras of Autumn* is persuasive, I want to make the case that it is in the poems whose visionary powers he most deprecates—those that follow in *The Rock*—that Stevens is finally able to embody his fiction. While "The Auroras of Autumn" is a speculation on the possibility of such a fiction, and "A Primitive Like an Orb" is, as Carroll terms it, "a definition with several illustrations,"[5] poems such as "The Rock" and "The Plain Sense of Things" depend on the supreme fiction as intertext for their full significance, although this has not been generally recognized. My distinction is between the earlier poems' specifications, definitions, or speculations in regard to a supreme fiction and the later poems' assumption of its actual presence, a fiction now functioning paradoxically as the belief or "reality" that lies behind the poems.

Stevens' fiction, of course, depends on such a paradox. In a memorandum of 1940 concerning a chair of poetry, he wrote, "The major poetic idea in the world is and always has been the idea of God" (*Letters* 378). A few months earlier he had written to Hi Simons that the "extreme poet will produce a poem equivalent to the idea of God." In explicating a section of "Owl's Clover," he states further,

> If one no longer believes in God (as truth), it is not possible merely to disbelieve; it becomes necessary to believe in something else. Logically, I ought to believe in essential imagination, but that has its difficulties. It is easier to believe in a thing created by the imagination. . . . In one of the short poems that I have just sent to the *Harvard Advocate* ["Asides on the Oboe"], I say that one's final belief must be in a fiction. I think that the history of belief will show that it has always been in a fiction. Yet the statement seems a negation, or, rather, a paradox. (*Letters* 370)

More than a decade later Stevens modeled his supreme fiction on the idea of God—not as a heavenly god, but as a god of reality might be. The fiction is not the human imagination itself but something created by it and modeled on it. Stevens' final fiction is a fusion of the idea of God and the idea of the imagination, or the idea of God as a purely aesthetic principle, the supreme imagination, although that is to put it somewhat too simply, since it is neither God nor imagination as these are normally conceived.

Stevens toyed with the idea of God (softened to "the gods") as a purely aesthetic figure in "Two or Three Ideas," a paper he read at a meeting of the College English Association in 1951. Here he conceives of the gods not as objects of belief but as "aesthetic projections" (*OP* 260). And when their time was over, "it was a time when their aesthetic had become invalid in the presence not of a greater aesthetic of the same kind, but of a different aesthetic" (*OP* 264). "A poem is a restricted creation of the imagination," he states. "The gods are the creation of the imagination at its utmost." And he notes finally that "we use the same faculties when we write poetry that we use when we create gods" (*OP* 266). At the time Stevens delivered these pronouncements he had already written in "Final Soliloquy of the Interior Paramour," "We say God and the imagination are one"—a line, however, sufficiently ambiguous to veil its more fanciful implications.

The merging of God and the imagination is treated playfully in "Credences of Summer," from the 1947 volume *Transport to Summer*. In 1942, "Notes" had spoken enigmatically of the existence of a "muddy centre before we breathed," "a myth before the myth began, / Venerable and articulate and complete" (383), suggesting that Stevens had earlier confronted the idea of a non-human mythic reality of some order. There are fainter and more debatable examples in even earlier poems—the "nothing that is" of "The Snow Man," for example. But as Stevens himself recognized, "Credences of Summer" signals the most obvious shift from the privileging of the human imagination in the early poems (and in "Notes") toward an attempt to articulate a reality independent of the observer's mind. "From the imaginative period of the Notes I turned to the ideas of Credences of Summer," Stevens said (*Letters* 636), and this tendency persisted though the remainder of his later poetry. Speaking of "An Ordinary Evening in New Haven" (from *The Auroras of Autumn*), he said, "This is not in any sense a turning away from the ideas of Credences of Summer: it is a development of those ideas" (*Letters* 637). To the poet Charles Tomlinson, Stevens wrote of "Credences," "At the time when that poem was written my feeling for the necessity of a final accord with reality was at its strongest: reality was the summer of the title of the book in which the poem appeared" (*Letters* 719). One of the many paradoxes of Stevens' later use of the supreme fiction is that it appears almost always in conjunction with attempts to posit a reality independent of the poet's imagination.

This is indeed the case in "Credences of Summer" (*CP* 372), which depicts a reality so entirely self-contained, "Complete in a completed scene," that the individual imagination is inoperative in the face of it, in "exile" in the poem's language. The singers of canto VII are forced to turn away from such a reality to sing "their unreal songs": "It was difficult to sing in face / Of the object. The singers had to avert themselves / Or else avert the object." It is a reality beyond the mind, beyond analysis, of which the speaker says, "Let's see the very thing and nothing else. / Let's see it with the hottest fire of sight," a seeing "Without evasion by a single metaphor." In "Credences" Stevens posits a summer world in which the sound of a morning bird "is not part of the listener's own sense."

It is in this context that he introduces his fiction of reality as a cosmic imagination. Throughout the poem Stevens has found ways of calling attention to the physical presence of the objects of summer. They are things to be seen, the gold sun, the tower, the rock that "cannot be broken," a mountain, "the visible announced" that is "the successor of the invisible." Yet at the poem's conclusion these solid objects become the fiction of an "inhuman author." They are "personae," costumed "characters," who are merely "speaking their parts" in a "completed scene":

> The personae of summer play the characters
> Of an inhuman author, who meditates
> With the gold bugs, in blue meadows, late at night.
> He does not hear his characters talk. He sees
> Them mottled, in the moodiest costumes,
>
> Of blue and yellow, sky and sun, belted
> And knotted, sashed and seamed, half pales of red,
> Half pales of green, appropriate habit for
> The huge decorum, the manner of the time,
> Part of the mottled mood of summer's whole,
>
> In which the characters speak because they want
> To speak, the fat, the roseate characters,
> Free, for a moment, from malice and sudden cry,

Complete in a completed scene, speaking
Their parts as in a youthful happiness.

Readers of the poem have had difficulty with this concluding canto, in large part because they ignore the implications of its fiction of the inhuman author. Harold Bloom believes it is "the poem's most problematic canto," but that is because he mistakenly determines that Stevens sees *himself* as the inhuman author and is thus forced to offer an explanation for "inhuman": "Stevens means something like 'not yet wholly human,' that is, not yet knowing himself wholly, beyond illusion." Joseph Riddel and Helen Vendler also mistake Stevens' reference to the inhuman author as a reference to himself, producing distorted readings. For Riddel, this means that in the end, the "physical [is] re-posed in the order of mind"; that is, the reality of summer is dissolved into the poet's imagination. Vendler's exemplary and influential reading goes wrong only with the final canto, which she believes begins "with the poet as a deliberate and distant manipulator of marionettes." Such a move is "Stevens' desperate, if truthful, expedient with which to end the poem."[6]

Stevens' inhuman author is perhaps an expedient, but it is relatively easy to show that he is not to be identified with the poet; the true difficulty of the final canto is to fathom why this author only *sees* his characters and does not hear them talk. David Jarraway confuses the issue by assuming that it is the "speeches" of the personae of summer that the inhuman author meditates, and that this undermines the poem's conclusion: the "'inhuman author' . . . is somewhat absurdly given to meditate their speeches 'late at night' even though he cannot hear them, much less see them."[7] But the poem says something more fanciful—that it is the objects of summer themselves that comprise the inhuman author's thought. They are what he thinks *with* (he "meditates / With the gold bugs"). He sees his characters and does not hear them talk because the poem has identified reality with the visible and the unreal with language, which is once removed from reality, as are the "unreal songs" of the singers of canto VII. In the fiction of the poem, reality is the *visible* meditation of a cosmic mind, and the objects of reality are the means by which this mind meditates. In the trope within this fiction, reality is also like a text, in that material objects are in fact playing roles dictated by the author who produced them. They are free to speak because their speech is not seen as a part of the reality meditated by their inhuman author, whose imagination operates with the visible, the blue and yellow and green of sky and sun and earth. Their speech is a sign of their sense of being "for a moment" free from "malice," freed from the exigencies of their "parts," in the same way that summer has been seen throughout the poem as a momentary sense of complete satisfaction, a moment of freedom from time in which "the mind lays by its trouble."

But does such a conception not undermine the entire poem, in which reality is not to be evaded by a single metaphor, not to mention the elaborate fiction of an inhuman author who meditates with gold bugs? To understand the place of the final canto in the poem as a whole, it is useful to read it against other passages in Stevens that adopt similar strategies. In all these instances the fiction of the supreme imagination addresses one difficulty while creating others. What it addresses is Stevens' attempt, toward the end of his career, to discover a way of representing poetically a separate and independent reality that is something more than the "muddy centre" of "Notes." The difficulties that it creates are perhaps obvious even from the example of "Credences of Summer," but chief among them are the contradictions it appears to engender and the misreadings it has produced. The *concept* of the supreme fiction in Stevens has been much better understood than his attempts to realize it.

The principal contradiction, which Stevens recognized and labeled a mere "paradox" (*Letters* 370), is a variation on his concept of a fiction "recognized as a fiction, in which men could propose to themselves a fulfillment" (*Letters* 820). In other words, the recognition of one's belief as a fiction does not impede its sufficiency as a fulfillment or sanction. Similarly, in "Credences of Summer" and throughout the late poems Stevens the poet imagines reality as the imagination of a mind independent of the poet. It could not in fact be independent of the poet who imagines it (any more than the poet's fiction could be real), but this difficulty does not apparently curb the efficacy of Stevens' fiction. His personae find satisfaction and ultimately fulfillment in a fiction "recognized as a fiction," in which, in his ambiguous phrasing, "the absence of the imagination had / Itself to be imagined." One of the several meanings of this paradox from "The Plain Sense of Things" (although not its primary meaning, as we will see) is that Stevens' fiction of an independent imagination is not simply a playful expedient. It is a necessity; it *has* to be imagined. Any attempt by the poet to depict a reality independent of his depiction would encounter the same paradox. Portraying that reality as itself an imagination, however, sharpens the sense of paradox, recognizes it as a fiction.

"Credences of Summer" and "The Auroras of Autumn" (*CP* 411) have frequently been read as companion poems—"the same day seen from two perspectives," Vendler says[8]—and one of the components they share is the fiction of the cosmic imagination. In "The Auroras of Autumn," as in the earlier poem, it makes its appearance near the end, and its primary function is to offer a fictional solution to the problem the poem has formulated. In "Credences" the problem was to imagine a pure and luminous reality independent of the human imagination; the solution, necessarily paradoxical, was to create the fiction of reality as the contents of a pure and brilliant *external* imagination, independent of the human, the imagination of an "inhuman author." The problem in "Auroras" is much more difficult to resolve, since the poem is not about the realization of such moments of complete luminosity and satisfaction but the breaking down of such moments and the dissolution of the fictions or ideas that produced them.

If "Credences" is about stasis, a moment "Beyond which there is nothing left of time," "Auroras" is about flux, a reality in which one is continually saying "Farewell to an idea"—the phrase that begins cantos II, III, and IV. In each of these cantos a point of order is dissolved: the ancestral house in II, the domestic comforts of the mother in III, and the fictions of the father in IV. These three motifs are brought together in canto V, when the mother "invites humanity to her house / And table" and the father "fetches tellers of tales and musicians." But this attempt to impose order degenerates into a "loud, disordered mooch," and by the end of canto VI it would appear that all ideas of order, all sustaining fictions, have been obliterated. The source of these fictions, the human imagination seen as a single candle, is ludicrously ineffectual against a destructive universe in flux, seen as the aurora borealis. The antithesis of the complete happiness of "Credences" is the total fear of "Auroras," the speaker's sense of an overwhelming and destructive universe: "He opens the door of his house / On flames."

> The scholar of one candle sees
> An Arctic effulgence flaring on the frame
> Of everything he is. And he feels afraid.

The poem cannot go further in this direction, and it is here that the supreme imagination of its companion poem makes its appearance.

The aurora borealis of the title is, interestingly, both the problem to be addressed and its solution. It represents a relentlessly destructive universe that, Dylan Thomas–like, kills everything it brings into being:

> It leaps through us, through all our heavens leaps,
> Extinguishing our planets, one by one,
> Leaving, of where we were and looked, of where
>
> We knew each other and of each other thought,
> A shivering residue. . . .

But in another version of "Death is the mother of beauty" (in "Sunday Morning"), it also represents what Stevens calls "An innocence of the earth and no false sign / Or symbol of malice." The auroras of autumn, that is, represent the universe as a cosmic genius who "meditates" things into and out of existence not maliciously but innocently, on a purely aesthetic basis, because he wants to experience vicariously all the lives that he imagines,

> The vital, the never-failing genius,
> Fulfilling his meditations, great and small.
>
> In these unhappy he meditates a whole,
> The full of fortune and the full of fate,
> As if he lived all lives, that he might know. . . .

Unlike the more elusive inhuman author of "Credences of Summer," the cosmic imagination of "The Auroras of Autumn" is depicted too unambiguously to be confused with the imagination of the poet. The fiction is, however, first introduced tentatively, as if the poet refused to take full responsibility for such an outrageous notion. Later, in the poems of *The Rock,* he will find other devices to soften its impact, such as his ploy in "Looking across the Fields and Watching the Birds Fly" of attributing the theory to the Emerson-like Mr. Homburg of Concord. Here, he cushions its introduction by presenting it as a series of questions:

> Is there an imagination that sits enthroned
> As grim as it is benevolent, the just
> And the unjust, which in the midst of summer stops
>
> To imagine winter? When the leaves are dead,
> Does it take its place in the north and enfold itself,
> Goat-leaper, crystalled and luminous, sitting
>
> In highest night? And do these heavens adorn
> And proclaim it, the white creator of black, jetted
> By extinguishings, even of planets as may be,
>
> Even of earth, even of sight, in snow,
> Except as needed by way of majesty,
> In the sky, as crown and diamond cabala?

By the end of the canto, however, the questions have reverted to statements, and the fiction of the universe as a cosmic imagination that creates seasons by stopping in the midst of summer to imagine winter is firmly established in the poem and in the remainder of Stevens' later poetry.[9]

Stevens plays with variations on the cosmic imagination in other poems of *The Auroras of Autumn.* In "The Ultimate Poem Is Abstract" (*CP* 429), a day about which the speaker cannot make up his mind is itself seen as mind, "an intellect / Of windings round and dodges to and fro, / Writhings in wrong obliques and distances." It is not, the speaker adds, "an intellect in which we are fleet"; rather, like the imagination of "The Auroras of Autumn," it is "present / Everywhere in space at once, cloud-pole / Of communication." In "Large Red Man Reading" (*CP* 423) ghosts from heaven return to earth to hear the mythical figure of the title read from "the poem of life," which, we are led to understand, is the ordinary reality—"the pans above the stove, the pots on the table"—that they have lacked. As he reads, the words become the physical objects themselves: "the literal characters, the vatic lines, / . . . Took on color, took on shape and size of things as they are." In "Puella Parvula" (*CP* 456), autumn is the triumph of "the mighty imagination," and the speaker asks his own mind to "Hear what he says, / The dauntless master, as he starts the human tale." In canto XXX of "An Ordinary Evening in New Haven" (*CP* 465), autumn is "a visibility of thought, / In which hundreds of eyes, in one mind, see at once." The poem concludes, "It is not in the premise that reality / Is a solid. It may be a shade that traverses / A dust, a force that traverses a shade." In the penultimate poem of the volume, "Things of August" (*CP* 489), the concept of reality as mind is again introduced as a series of questions: "The world? The inhuman as human? That which thinks not, / Feels not, resembling thought, resembling feeling?"

Joseph Carroll, as I have noted, finds the supreme fiction present in two other poems of the volume, "The Owl in the Sarcophagus" and "A Primitive like an Orb," but these, although clearly visionary poems, present very different fictions from the one I am tracing here. "The Owl in the Sarcophagus" (*CP* 431) is a deeply-felt but failed attempt to create what it calls "the mythology of modern death" by inventing (somewhat crudely) human figures for sleep, peace after death, and the memory of the dead. "A Primitive like an Orb" (*CP* 440) tackles an issue related to the cosmic imagination, an abstraction that Stevens calls the "essential poem" or the "central poem," whose existence cannot be proven: "It is something seen and known in lesser poems."

The concept that informs "A Primitive like an Orb" is much less daring than the fiction of reality as inhuman imagination. Although at some points in the poem Stevens mythologizes the concept by picturing it as a giant ("an abstraction given head / . . . given arms, / A massive body and long legs"), at other points it appears to be no more than a version of Eliot's notion in "Tradition and the Individual Talent" that all existing works of art together form an ideal order, an abstraction complete in itself but changed slightly by the addition of each new work. In the final stanza of the poem Stevens suggests that each artist, of whatever art, is a "part" of "the total of letters, prophecies, perceptions, clods of color." And earlier he had defined the central poem as "the poem of the whole, / the poem of the composition of the whole." It is

> the miraculous multiplex of lesser poems,
> Not merely into a whole, but the poem of
> The whole, the essential compact of the parts,
> The roundness that pulls tight the final ring. . . .

The concept of art contained in "A Primitive like an Orb" is not unlike the idea introduced in Stevens' 1951 paper, "The Relations between Poetry and Painting," and attributed to Baudelaire—"that there exists an unascertained and fundamental aesthetic, or order, of which poetry and painting are manifestations, but of which, for that matter, sculpture or music or any other aesthetic realization would equally be a manifestation" (*NA* 160). Such a notion—that "One poem proves another and the whole," as Stevens puts it in "A Primitive"—is at best a minor fiction or simply a way of conceiving of the relation of each work of art to the totality of art. Although it bears some relation to the more fantastic fiction Stevens was elaborating at the same time, it is this latter fiction, reality as cosmic imagination, that serves as one of the essential intertexts for the final collection, *The Rock*.

By the time of *The Rock* this fiction has become pervasive. The great majority of the poems of *The Rock* and a number of other poems written at about the same time (and collected in *Opus Posthumous*) depend on it in various ways. In the latter group are poems written in 1954 and 1955—"Presence of an External Master of Knowledge," "Reality Is an Activity of the Most August Imagination," "Artificial Populations," "A Clear Day and No Memories"— whose titles are sufficient to suggest its presence. This is true as well of one of the key poems of *The Rock*, "The World as Meditation" (*CP* 520), whose epigraph (from the composer Georges Enesco) states in part, "Je vis un rêve permanent, qui ne s'arrête ni nuit ni jour."

An uncollected poem of 1950, "Nuns Painting Water-Lilies" (*OP* 120), concludes, "We are part of a fraicheur, inaccessible / Or accessible only in the most furtive fiction." Stevens' fiction is indeed furtive in many of the poems of *The Rock*, accessible only in the figures and images of poems such as "A Quiet Normal Life," "Long and Sluggish Lines," and "One of the Inhabitants of the West." It is, however, overtly described in others—"The Rock," "The World as Meditation," and "Looking across the Fields and Watching the Birds Fly," to take the three most obvious examples. In the first section of "The Rock" (*CP* 525), the speaker conceives of the events of his life as the "invention" of a "fantastic consciousness"; in "Looking across the Fields" (*CP* 517), an afternoon is "Too much like thinking to be less than thought"; in "The World as Meditation" Penelope senses "an inhuman meditation, larger than her own."

In the following chapters I will examine these poems and others as specimens of Stevens' final fiction of the world as inhuman meditation, but for the moment I want to suggest some of the implications of its presence in *The Rock* by reading it as the intertext of one of the least likely candidates of the volume, "The Plain Sense of

Things" (*CP* 502). It is the poem that Joseph Carroll reads as "an end of the visionary process," an indication that "Stevens' 'fantastic effort' to create a supreme fiction has failed to fix itself in a permanent realization."[10] I want to demonstrate the way in which the poem, to the contrary, depends for its significance on the presence of the supreme fiction, or at least a version of it. And since one of the qualities of the supreme fiction is that it must change, no formulation could be more than a "version."

Carroll's negative reading of the poem depends on his assumption (the general assumption of readers of the poem) that the third stanza's failed "fantastic effort" is Stevens' own. He assumes, moreover, that the plain sense of things is Stevens' own sense, "and that it discloses itself as a sense of imaginative inanition." The poem thus becomes an account of Stevens' "imaginative impotence," and the "inevitable knowledge" of the final stanza is the poet's knowledge of the emptiness to which his earlier Romantic vision has been reduced.[11] But such a reading ignores the central insight of the poem—that "the absence of the imagination had / Itself to be imagined"—and it ignores as well Stevens' characterization of the imaginative effort the poem describes as "fantastic." Most crucially, it ignores the poem's ambiguity of agency.

Like many of the poems of *The Rock*, "The Plain Sense of Things" is careful not to ascribe the plain sense or the failed imagination to the speaker or to any specific agent. It begins,

> After the leaves have fallen, we return
> To a plain sense of things. It is as if
> We had come to an end of the imagination,
> Inanimate in an inert savoir.

Whose plain sense of things is it to which we return? And whose lack of imagination and inert savoir do we come to, or come upon? Although the second sentence has been read as a statement about the condition of the poet's imagination, the "as if" of the second line indicates the presence of a poetic figure. It appears to be a variation of the central figure of "Note on Moonlight" (*CP* 531), also from *The Rock,* in which moonlight in a "simple-colored night" is seen as "a plain poet revolving in his mind / The sameness of his various universe." If reality is conceived of as the thought of such a poet, or as the "inhuman meditation" of "The World as Meditation" or the "pensive nature" of "Looking across the Fields and Watching the Birds Fly," then winter can be thought of as a particular state of mind of that consciousness. It is as if winter is such a mind's plain sense of things, its lack of imagination. Winter necessarily represents such a mind's knowledge, even imagination, as we learn later in the poem, but now it appears inanimate, inert. The first two lines of the poem, in which the "plain sense of things" is associated with the fallen leaves, also appear to contain as intertext the description of the cosmic imagination in "The Auroras of Autumn," which conceives its winter world "When the leaves are dead."[12]

If we read the poem as responding to its intertext of Stevens' fiction of the inhuman imagination, many of its figures begin to take on a new sense. The second stanza begins, "It is difficult even to choose the adjective / For this blank cold, this sadness without cause." Here, "this sadness without cause" is clearly in apposition to "this blank cold"; it is not the speaker's sadness but the weather's. Moreover, to think of winter's cold as "blank" is to suggest that the inhuman author who created it did not supply its adjective or description. And it is important to note that the speaker, unlike the cosmic imagination, *is* able to fill in the blank with a succession of imaginative figures:

> The great structure has become a minor house.
> No turban walks across the lessened floors.
>
> The greenhouse never so badly needed paint.
> The chimney is fifty years old and slants to one side.
> A fantastic effort has failed, a repetition
> In a repetitiousness of men and flies.

There is apparently nothing wrong with the poet-speaker's own imagination, as is testified to by the poem as a whole. The "fantastic effort" that has failed belongs not to the poet, as has been assumed, but to the imagination that, in the poem's fiction, creates summer, its yearly "repetition / In a repetitiousness of men and flies." Neither the repetition nor the flies make sense in reference to the poet's own imagination; the "fantastic effort" was the creation of summer, which now appears to have failed. It is "fantastic" in the same sense as the "fantastic consciousness" of "The Rock," conceived by unrestrained fancy, so outrageous as to challenge belief.[13] The poem, in short, plays a variation on the enthroned imagination of "The Auroras of Autumn," which "in the midst of summer stops / To imagine winter." This imagination, however, initially gives the impression not so much of imagining winter as of failing to imagine it, although the speaker later corrects himself when he recognizes that "the absence of the imagination had / Itself to be imagined."

These lines, which begin the penultimate stanza, have naturally been read as referring to the poet's own imagination, to suggest, as Anthony Whiting puts it, that "the imagining of the absence of the imagination is itself a powerful expression of the creative activity of the imagination."[14] This sense of the paradox is certainly present, as I suggested earlier. It is in part Stevens' recognition of the quandary into which his late conception of an external imagination has led him. Yet to read the lines in the context of the poem's conclusion as a whole suggests another reading, which was implicit from the beginning—that is, even what appears initially to be an absence must necessarily be a presence, at least in terms of the poem's fiction. If the speaker is true to this fiction, then even the pond "without reflections," the leaves, mud, and water, and "the waste of the lilies" must themselves have been thought into being by the inhuman meditation to which everything in the winter scene is attributed:

> Yet the absence of the imagination had
> Itself to be imagined. The great pond,
> The plain sense of it, without reflections, leaves,
> Mud, water like dirty glass, expressing silence

Of a sort, silence of a rat come out to see,
The great pond and its waste of the lilies, all this
Had to be imagined as an inevitable knowledge,
Required, as a necessity requires.

The ambiguity of agency is maintained ingeniously through the two stanzas' use of the infinitive "to be"; the speaker avoids a construction that attributes the imagination or the knowledge to himself. His discovery is their inevitability, their necessity. Why does the imagination *have to be* an "inevitable knowledge," and why is it required "as a necessity"? It would appear that Stevens wants to suggest (although not too clearly) that the mood of winter is a mental act, an external knowledge, operating according to some necessary principle. Winter is not the absence of the imagination that created summer, as it first appeared, but a different imaginative act, one required by the necessity through which the inhuman imagination operates in Stevens' larger fiction.[15]

"The Plain Sense of Things" is in part a reworking of canto XXX of "An Ordinary Evening in New Haven," and reading the two together throws some light on both poems.

The wind has blown the silence of summer away.
It buzzes beyond the horizon or in the ground:
In mud under ponds, where the sky used to be reflected.

The barrenness that appears is an exposing.
It is not part of what is absent, a halt
For farewells, a sad hanging on for remembrances.

It is a coming on and a coming forth.
The pines that were fans and fragrances emerge,
Staked solidly in a gusty grappling with rocks.

The glass of the air becomes an element—
It was something imagined that has been washed away.
A clearness has returned. It stands restored.

It is not an empty clearness, a bottomless sight.
It is a visibility of thought,
In which hundreds of eyes, in one mind, see at once.

Expression such as "something imagined" and "a visibility of thought" in "An Ordinary Evening" preserve the same kind of ambiguity as in the later "Plain Sense of Things." The insight here is also that of the later poem—that what appears as an absence, a lack, is in fact "a coming forth," a clarity of mind, "a visibility of thought," although a mind and a visibility not a part of the speaker's own sense. The canto's conclusion again evokes Stevens' fiction of reality as the visualization of inhuman thought, "In which hundreds of eyes, in one mind, see at once."

In "Some Reflections on Intertexuality," Barbara Johnson notes that when a work is read intertextually it "becomes differently energized, traversed by forces and desires that are invisible or unreadable to those who see it as an independent homogeneous message unit."[16] Among the consequences of reading Stevens' late poems as having absorbed his fiction of the supreme imagination is the recognition both of the extent to which they are intratextual commentaries on each other and the whole, and of the extent to which they are traversed by forces otherwise unreadable.[17] The last line of "Not Ideas about the Thing but the Thing Itself" (CP 534) provides an interesting illustration, especially because of its position as the last line and thus the last word of the Collected Poems.

The poem is set "At the earliest ending of winter," and it begins with "a scrawny cry from outside," a bird's song "at daylight or before," which initially seems to be a sound in the speaker's mind. The struggle of the poem is to push it outside: "It would have been outside. / . . . / The sun was coming from outside." Like many of Stevens' late poems, it is an attempt to grant external reality—here only the faintest of sounds—an independent existence, free from his own mind: "It was not from the vast ventriloquism / Of sleep's faded papier-mâché." The poem ends,

That scrawny cry—it was
A chorister whose c preceded the choir.
It was part of the colossal sun,

Surrounded by its choral rings,
Still far away. It was like
A new knowledge of reality.

If the poem is read independently, outside its context in *The Rock,*
it is a poem about the speaker's new knowledge of reality. Read
intertextually, it is a poem about the coming of spring as itself a
new knowledge of reality. The trope is appropriately bold; it is not
the speaker's knowledge but a new season as a new knowledge, not
ideas *about* the thing but the thing itself. The *it,* which occurs three
times in the passage and six times in the poem, always refers to the
bird's cry, as it does in the final sentence. It is the bird's scrawny cry,
from *outside,* evoking the sound of a newborn baby, that is like a
new knowledge of reality. It is Stevens' final version of the final fic-
tion, a supreme imagination that awakens at the end of winter to
imagine spring.

2 / Schopenhauer and the Two Worlds of *The Rock*

There is always an analogy between nature and the imagination, and possibly
poetry is merely the strange rhetoric of that parallel. . . .
—STEVENS, "Effects of Analogy"

STEVENS' PLACEMENT OF "Not Ideas about the Thing but the
Thing Itself" with its last line—"A new knowledge of reality"—at
the end of *The Rock* is as deliberate as the placement of *The Rock*'s
opening poem, "An Old Man Asleep." "Not Ideas about the Thing"
(*CP* 534) was almost certainly the last of the *Collected Poems* to be
composed (see *Letters* 835 n. 7);[1] it also brings to a conclusion a sea-
sonal motif in *The Rock* that had begun "After the leaves have
fallen" and arrives now "At the earliest ending of winter." In "An Old
Man Asleep" (*CP* 501) "two worlds" are asleep, and in the conclud-
ing poem both worlds are waking. Perhaps more significantly, "Not
Ideas about the Thing" addresses an ambiguously depicted rela-
tionship between the two worlds that Stevens had introduced in the
opening lines of *The Rock* and had contemplated throughout the
section.

In "An Old Man Asleep" these worlds are named "The self and
the earth." They are in some sense (not fully apparent) parallel, and
they constitute the explicit subject of the poem and the implicit
subject of *The Rock* as a whole.

The two worlds are asleep, are sleeping, now.
A dumb sense possesses them in a kind of solemnity.

The self and the earth—your thoughts, your feelings,
Your beliefs and disbeliefs, your whole peculiar plot;

The redness of your reddish chestnut trees,
The river motion, the drowsy motion of the river R.

The poem initiates one of the key stylistic features of *The Rock,* an ambiguity of reference that at times makes it impossible to say with certainty to whom or what pronouns refer or to whom or what particular actions or qualities are attributed. The poem begins as a third-person description of the two worlds of self and earth and then switches abruptly to the second person. On first reading it appears that the *yours* all refer to the self—"your thoughts, your feelings, / Your beliefs and disbeliefs"—but are "your reddish chestnut trees" those of the self or of the earth?[2] Clearly "the drowsy motion of the river R" of the last line belongs to the earth, or does it? As Eleanor Cook has pointed out, the poem ends with a pun on the river R (are), the river of being in which the self is contained, much like "The River of Rivers in Connecticut" near the conclusion of the section. The drowsy motion of the river of being is thus fused with the drowsiness of the old man of the title, but the title itself has a double reference, since, as Cook also notes from a different perspective, Old Man River is a conventional association.[3] Is the drowsiness of the river a projection of the old man's drowsiness, or is it the opposite, a human drowsiness engendered by "the drowsy motion of the river R"? The poem's second line suggests an alternative explanation. The two worlds, it states, are both possessed by a "dumb sense," are themselves contained in something larger, a knowledge or sense, or even a narrative of sorts (as the fourth line suggests). Ever alert for wordplay, Eleanor Cook has overlooked the key instance in the poem: "your thoughts, your feelings," the speaker says, addressing the unidentified possessor of the two worlds, "Your beliefs and disbeliefs, your whole peculiar plot." The word "plot" is indeed peculiar, since it signifies at once the landscape of the chestnut trees and river and the narrative or scheme that encloses the thoughts, feelings, and beliefs. And if the landscape is indeed a plot, something imagined or planned, then it is clear why the speaker's drowsiness parallels "the drowsy motion of the river R," since the river of being is itself conceived as a sense, a knowledge. In the trope of the poem, the earth is the dumb sense of an old man asleep.

Parallel worlds make other appearances in *The Rock*, although they are not always so easily labeled as the self and earth of "An Old Man Asleep." The most celebrated instance is "To an Old Philosopher in Rome" (*CP* 508), in which the dying Santayana inhabits two worlds,

> The threshold, Rome, and that more merciful Rome
> Beyond, the two alike in the make of the mind.
> It is as if in a human dignity
> Two parallels become one, a perspective, of which
> Men are part both in the inch and in the mile.

The title of "The World as Meditation" suggests another kind of parallel between the self and the earth, a world modeled on the workings of the mind, while "Looking across the Fields and Watching the Birds Fly" (*CP* 517) theorizes the simultaneous existence of an alien element, "free / From man's ghost, larger and yet a little like" in which "we live beyond ourselves in air." Two other examples will perhaps suffice to suggest the degree to which this motif permeates *The Rock*. The title poem (*CP* 525) postulates two parallel "cures" for the nothingness of being, "a cure of the ground / Or a cure of ourselves," and the two seem roughly equivalent to what Stevens had earlier labeled the self and the earth. In "Final Soliloquy of the Interior Paramour" (*CP* 524), the speaker is able to forget the human self in the presence of something larger but again modeled on the form of human intelligence:

> Here, now, we forget each other and ourselves.

We feel the obscurity of an order, a whole,
A knowledge, that which arranged the rendezvous.

It is within the "vital boundary" of the larger parallel world than the speaker is able to say that "God and the imagination are one."

To return to "Not Ideas about the Thing" with these poems in mind, we see that, without being named explicitly, the two worlds evident throughout *The Rock* are present here also and that the speaker's epiphany is the recognition of the separate existence of the external world, the world of a bird's scrawny cry. As Robert Pogue Harrison has pointed out in a perceptive reading of the poem, one of the means by which it grants a separate existence to the external is to acknowledge its "earliness." The time is "the earliest ending of winter" in "early March," "at daylight or before." The bird's cry is a chorister's *c* which "preceded the choir." The poem, in Harrison's words, "places us at the heart of the inconceivable priority of nature"[4] in the speaker's recognition that the "outside," although it resembles the "inside," does not depend upon it. The moment of this recognition is, paradoxically, not one of vitality or strength but of weakness, and this is true of such moments throughout *The Rock*. As in the opening poem of the section, it is the speaker's drowsiness, his incomplete recovery from "sleep's faded papier-mâché," that Stevens associates with the granting of independence to a larger world that appears to possess a knowledge of its own. The linking of the speaker's old age, weakness, infirmity, and poverty with his vital insights about the relationship of the self and the earth is a part of the fiction that the poems of *The Rock* have absorbed. The link, however, is not fixed nor easy to delineate; it takes different forms, which appear at times to contradict one another.

On the one hand, it is as if the poet's own weakness, the poverty of his imagination, is evidence that the world he observes is not his own construct. The scrawny cry of "Not Ideas about the Thing" is a part of the sun's world, not his own. The external world is not *his* fiction, the product of *his* perspective, yet it retains its status as artifice of some order. It is of the same *nature* as his fiction, his perspective. It then follows, in the strange logic of *The Rock,* that this artifice must have another source. On the other hand, the parallel poverty of the external world, the scrawniness of its cry, is also seen as evidence of its separate existence in many of the poems, and these merit a closer look.

In "A Quiet Normal Life" (*CP* 523) the frailty of the scene in which the speaker finds himself—the fact that it is so badly lit, shadowed—is linked without explanation to the awareness that it is not of his own making:

> His place, as he sat and as he thought, was not
> In anything that he constructed, so frail,
> So barely lit, so shadowed over and naught. . . .

Although the connection is not made explicit, the implication is that the lack of imaginative detail in the scene, its drabness, shows that it is not a construct of his imagination. Indeed, it appears that the entire scene, himself included, is the construct of a "gallant" but inadequate imagination—gallant presumably in asserting itself even in its weakness. It is as if he had come upon

> a world in which, like snow,
> He became an inhabitant, obedient
> To gallant notions on the part of cold.

The emptiness ("naught") of the scene is compared to the nothing-ness of snow, and snow, in turn, is conceived as an idea *on the part of* cold. The odd phrasing is necessary to make clear that snow is not simply synonymous with coldness. Cold is an entity capable of gallant notions, and snow is one of them. The speaker is like snow because he has the sense of being an inhabitant of the scene, not its creator, obedient to that which created it in much the same manner as the speaker of the following poem ("Final Soliloquy of the Interior Paramour") curbs his own will in the presence of "that which arranged the rendezvous." In both poems, as in "Not Ideas about the Thing," the external world is given priority; the speaker is a latecomer.

Stevens plays with the possessive pronoun throughout "A Quiet Normal Life." *His* place, it turns out, is not quite his.

> It was here. This was the setting and the time
> Of year. Here in his house and in his room,
> In his chair, the most tranquil thought grew peaked
>
> And the oldest and the warmest heart was cut
> By gallant notions on the part of night—
> Both late and alone, above the crickets' chords,
>
> Babbling, each one, the uniqueness of its sound.
> There was no fury in transcendent forms.
> But his actual candle blazed with artifice.

Just as snow is "obedient / To gallant notions on the part of cold," he is obedient to "gallant notions on the part of night." He is an inhabitant of a world without "transcendent forms" which is, at the same time, an artifact. The poem strains to hold together two seemingly contradictory perspectives. The moment is ordinary—an old man sits alone late at night in his house, his room, his chair, in a scene from a "quiet normal life." Yet the very poverty of the scene produces an extraordinary recognition in which "the most tranquil thought grew peaked" and "the warmest heart was cut." Candles most frequently suggest the imagination to Stevens, but here he insists that it is his "actual candle" that "blazed with artifice." That is, the candle is not to be read merely as a sign for something else, a conventional symbol of the speaker's imaginative construction of the scene. It is a real candle and he is not the source of its artifice.

Stevens, in fact, takes great pains here to prevent conventional misreadings that would assign the candle and its artifice to his own imagination. The scene is not something that he has made; he is merely "an inhabitant, obedient" to notions on the part of something else; the candle is actual. His attempt to forestall misreadings has, however, proved unsuccessful. Edward Kessler believes the poem shows that the "imagination can heighten the actual candle," and Frank Doggett reads the candle as consciousness, which "blazes with created or fictive conception." Not knowing quite what to say about the poem, critics have paid it little attention. Charles Berger's Bloomian reading is the most ambitious. He sees it as a poem of retraction in which Stevens casts doubts upon the value of his earlier poetry. The references to snow, he believes, allude to "The Snow Man," about which Stevens now expresses reservations. The poem ends with Stevens' pride in his artifice, although it "leaves us with the sense of a poet deriving little comfort from the fact that he has fashioned transcendent, or lasting, works of art." Berger's reading, while engaging, depends on our attributing to Stevens the transcendent forms (which are pointedly not present) and the artifice (which the speaker claims not to have created). Thomas Lombardi believes that the poem's title must be ironic since Stevens' life "at age seventy . . . is certainly far from 'Normal.'"[5]

The title is ironic but in a somewhat different sense. What the poem says is that the most unimaginative moment in the quietest and most normal life is, in the fiction of *The Rock,* a moment of artifice, although not of the speaker's own making, "not / In anything that he constructed." Stevens' assumptions buried in the poem (and thus far undetected) are first that what he has always called reality, in opposition to artifice, may itself be viewed as artifice, and further that this view is made plain once his own artifice, in the poverty of old age, is absent from the scene.

It is not, however, merely the poverty of his own sense of things that is revelatory, but the plain sense possessed by things—that is, a plainness of the external world that parallels the internal. This is suggested in a poem written in the same year as "A Quiet Normal Life" with the off-putting title "Lebensweisheitspielerei" (*CP* 504). The poem was first published in *The Nation* in 1952 in a group of seven short poems that included "An Old Man Asleep," "The Plain Sense of Things," and "The Green Plant." "Lebensweisheitspielerei," also passed over by Stevens' commentators, is in fact one of the more telling poems of *The Rock,* since it discloses a key intertext from Arthur Schopenhauer that is useful in deciphering the two worlds of the late poems.

The title is less arbitrary and more revealing than it may first appear. Thomas Lombardi says that it means "to play around with the wisdom of life," which is literally correct but incomplete, and William Burney's statement about the poem—"All one can do with that life-weary wisdom is play around, as the title . . . indicates"[6]— is misleading. First, *spielerei* does not necessarily have the negative connotations that "playing around" carries; it is often used in a positive sense, as it is in this poem, which is somber, does not by any means "play around." Further, *Lebensweisheit* suggests more than "the wisdom of life"; it indicates wisdom learned through the experience of a lifetime, as opposed to mere knowledge. Here the wisdom of the speaker's old age, in the "stale grandeur of annihilation," involves finally seeing life as it is, of perceiving the "finally human," as "Each person completey touches us / With what he is and as he is. . . ."

The phrasing, like the title, owes something to the poem's principal intertext, which is a translation of Schopenhauer that Stevens owned, *The Wisdom of Life: Being the First Part of Arthur Schopenhauer's Aphorismen zur Lebensweisheit*.[7] The *spielerei* of Stevens' title carries with it a sense of *aperçus* or aphorisms on the wisdom of life, as in Schopenhauer's title. "*Aperçus* of Life's Wisdom" would be an awkward but not inadequate translation,[8] since the poem implies that its insights are based on nothing more than common experience: "A look, a few words spoken." The poem also carries with it something of the modesty suggested by Schopenhauer's *Aphorismen*. In the "Translator's Preface" T. Bailey Saunders says of Schopenhauer's prose style in these essays,

> It must be recognised that the data are insufficient for large views, and that we ought not to go beyond the facts we have, the facts of ordinary life, interpreted by the common experience of every day. These form our only material. The views we take must of necessity be fragmentary; they can be little but *aperçus*, rough guesses at the undiscovered. (*Wisdom* xix)

It is of course with "the facts of ordinary life, interpreted by the common experience of every day," that "Lebensweisheitspielerei" and other poems of *The Rock* are concerned, as some of their titles ("A Quiet Normal Life," "The Plain Sense of Things") would indicate. Saunders notes of *The Wisdom of Life* that Schopenhauer "is content to call these witty and instructive pages a series of aphorisms; thereby indicating that he makes no claim to expound a complete theory of conduct" (*Wisdom* xxi).

From his earliest years as a reader Stevens had been attracted to aphoristic texts like those of Schopenhauer and Nietzsche. A journal entry of 1906 reads, "Have just finished Leopardi's 'Pensieri.' . . . They are paragraphs on human nature like Schopenhauer's psychological observations, Paschals [*sic*] 'Pensées,' Rochefoucauld's 'Maximes' etc. How true they all are! I should like to have a library of such things" (*Letters* 88). But there are a number of other qualities of *Aphorismen sur Lebensweisheit* (and Saunders' preface to it) that Stevens would have found equally engaging at the time he was working on the poems of *The Rock*. Saunders' translation of *Aphorismen zur Lebensweisheit* appeared as two separate volumes, *The Wisdom of Life* and *Counsels and Maxims*; although only the first is now in the Stevens Collection at the Huntington Library, both volumes appear to have been absorbed by the late poems. My interest in them is not as sources in the traditional sense, explanations of the origins of the poems, but as intertexts, aids in determining the significance of key elements of the poems.

Aphorismen zur Lebensweisheit differs markedly from Schopenhauer's major work, *Die Welt als Wille und Vorstellung,* in that it abandons the rigorous philosophical perspective of the earlier work and discusses, in Saunders' words, "the pleasures which a wise man will seek to obtain" (*Wisdom* xxi). It also abandons, for the most part, the pessimism of the earlier work. As Schopenhauer admits, these maxims represent a compromise. He notes in his introduction that although his subject is the means "of ordering our lives so as to obtain the greatest possible amount of pleasure and success," this premise "is based upon a fundamental mistake":

Accordingly, in elaborating the scheme of a happy existence, I have had to make a complete surrender of the higher metaphysical and ethical standpoint to which my own theories lead; and everything I shall say here will to some extent rest upon a compromise; in so far, that is, as I take the common standpoint of every day, and embrace the error which is at the bottom of it. (*Wisdom* 1-2)

The error that *The World as Will and Idea* had demonstrated is the assumption that a happy life could in fact be achieved.

Stevens would have discovered from Saunders' preface that the work was written toward the close of Schopenhauer's life and that it makes its appeal not to philosophical theory but to "the experience of common life" (*Wisdom* i, ii). The aged philosopher contemplating life, happiness, reputation, and fame corresponds to the stance Stevens sometimes assumes in *The Rock*, the poet looking back on his life and career "Seventy Years Later," as the title of the first section of "The Rock" has it. Stevens would have noted Saunders' claim that "Schopenhauer can be said to have brought down philosophy from heaven to earth" (*Wisdom* iv) in the way that he himself had attempted to write "the great poem of the earth" to succeed the "great poems of heaven and hell" already written (*NA* 142).

Stevens would have noted as well that Schopenhauer's two worlds of will and idea are not altogether different from the two worlds of *The Rock*. He would have recognized the likeness between his fiction of the cosmic imagination in the late poems—the world as modeled on human meditation—and Schopenhauer's concept of the world as will. In *The World as Will and Idea* Schopenhauer states that he has "shown the world as the macranthropos: because will and idea exhaust its nature as they do that of man." Thus it is "clearly more correct to learn to understand the world from man than man from the world," since the human will "is of all things the one that is known to us most exactly, the only thing given immediately, and therefore exclusively fitted for the explanation of the rest" (*World* 3:471-72). Although Stevens' fiction of the world as cosmic imagination is not identical to Schopenhauer's world as will, the two concepts agree in the most fundamental aspect—what Schopenhauer calls the world as "macranthropos," the human as the pattern for the external world as a whole. Schopenhauer is a direct presence in only a few poems of *The Rock,* but it is useful to look briefly at the manner in which his thought coincides, perhaps fortuitously in some cases, with that of Stevens.

In his preface to *The Wisdom of Life* Saunders introduces Schopenhauer's key concept by arguing that all philosophy is an attempt to discover a unifying principle:

> Schopenhauer conceived this unifying principle, this underlying unity, to consist in something analogous to that *will* which self-consciousness reveals to us. *Will* is, according to him, the fundamental reality of the world, the thing-in-itself; and its objectivation [*sic*] is what is presented in phenomena. The struggle of the will to realise itself evolves the organism, which in its turn evolves intelligence as the servant of the will. And in practical life the antagonism between the will and the intellect arises from the fact that the former is the metaphysical substance, the latter something accidental and secondary. (*Wisdom* iii)

But while Schopenhauer reads this concept and its larger implications as an occasion for pessimism, Stevens reads it (or something quite similar to it) in the opposite manner. One of the intriguing links between the two men is that they discern the same pattern at the heart of existence but interpret it in antithetical ways.

For Schopenhauer life is a constant assertion of the will, which is an "endless striving" (*World* 1:213), a desire never permanently satisfied, whose temporary satisfactions lead only to boredom:

> Eternal becoming, endless flux, characterises the revelation of the inner nature of will. Finally, the same thing shows itself in human endeavours and desires, which always delude us by presenting their satisfaction as the final end of will. As soon as we attain to them they no longer appear the same, and therefore they soon grow stale, are forgotten, and though not openly disowned, are yet always thrown aside as vanished illusions. (*World* 1:214)

So life is a "constant transition from desire to satisfaction, and from satisfaction to a new desire," since satisfaction is apt to "sink into that stagnation that shows itself in fearful ennui that paralyses life, vain yearning without a definite object, deadening languor" (*World* 1:215). Since Schopenhauer identifies unsatisfied desire with suffering, he concludes that "life swings like a pendulum backwards and forwards between pain and ennui" (*World* 1:402).

A cycle that oscillates between desire and ennui is of course the assumption that drives much of Stevens' poetry. Yet there is a crucial difference between his thought and that of Schopenhauer: for Stevens the cycle is the source of pleasure, not pain. In fact, many of Stevens' most characteristic poems may be read as refutations of the inference Schopenhauer draws from his system. It is true, they assume, that life fluctuates between desire and boredom. It is true that our desires can never be permanently satisfied. The "never resting mind" needs to escape "what has been so long composed" (*CP* 194). "It can never be satisfied, the mind, never" (*CP* 247). Yet this recognition is for Stevens the base of human happiness and the source of poetry. The model is most often the cycles of nature, as it is for the woman of "Sunday Morning" (*CP* 66), "her desire for June and evening, tipped / By the consummation of the swallow's wings." A world without the cycles of desire and consummation, without the occasion for new desires, would be a place of eternal boredom, like the heaven of stanza VI of "Sunday Morning." Schopenhauer would no doubt have agreed with this depiction of paradise, since he said that "after man had transferred all pain and torments to hell, there then remained nothing over for heaven but ennui" (*World* 1:402).

Stevens' most rigorous analysis of the cycles of desire and ennui occurs in canto II of the first section of "Notes toward a Supreme Fiction" (*CP* 380), where the speaker illustrates for the young poet the relation of poetry and desire. He has explained that it is "the celestial ennui of apartments / That sends us back to the first idea," to a fresh seeing, a new beginning, and the young poet has apparently asked if the first idea can in its turn become boring: "May there be an ennui of the first idea? / What else, prodigious scholar, should there be?" Even the philosopher, who "Appoints man's place" in his system, "desires":

> And not to have is the beginning of desire.
> To have what is not is its ancient cycle.
> It is desire at the end of winter, when
>
> It observes the effortless weather turning blue
> And sees the myosotis on its bush.
> Being virile, it hears the calendar hymn.
>
> It knows that what it has is what is not
> And throws it away like a thing of another time,
> As morning throws off stale moonlight and shabby sleep.

This is precisely Schopenhauer's description of the cycle: when we attain our desires "they soon grow stale" and are "thrown aside as vanished illusions." Schopenhauer's aim is thus to escape the cycle, and one means of doing so is through aesthetic contemplation: "Whenever it discloses itself suddenly to our view, it almost always succeeds in delivering us, though it may be only for a moment, from subjectivity, from the slavery of the will, and in raising us to the state of pure knowing" (*World* 1:255). Art plays a role in the cycle for Stevens as well, but its function is, conversely, to begin the cycle anew. As he puts it in "Notes," "The poem refreshes life so that we share, / For a moment, the first idea." The poem "satisfies / Belief in an immaculate beginning," but only for a moment, since Stevens recognizes as well as Schopenhauer that every fresh beginning is destined to grow stale, initiating new desires.

Yet if Stevens disagrees with Schopenhauer on the implications of his system in terms of human happiness, *late* Stevens at least would have found much in the system congenial, especially its tendency to project human consciousness as the model for the external world. The affinity between Schopenhauer's formulation of the world as will and idea and Stevens' fiction in the poems of *The Rock* becomes more conspicuous if we read them *as if* they contained an intertext from Schopenhauer. To read the final poem of *The Rock*, "Not Ideas about the Thing but the Thing Itself," for example, in light of Schopenhauer's concept of will is not to suggest Schopenhauer's influence but to recognize that the poem is based on an opposition between the two key terms of Schopenhauer's philosophy, the world as idea versus the world as will, the thing-in-itself. "The world is entirely idea," Schopenhauer writes, "and as such demands the knowing subject as the supporter of its existence" (*World* 1:38). But the "objective world, the world as idea, is not the only side of the world, but merely its outward side; and it has an entirely different side—the side of its inmost nature—its kernel—the thing-in-itself" (*World* 1:39). This is the world as will. In Schopenhauerean terms, the poem's motive is to establish the priority of the thing-in-itself, to suggest that the world of the bird's cry is a representation of a cosmic will, to acknowledge the secondariness of the human intellect, the world as idea.

Richard P. Adams, who assumes that Stevens read *The World as Will and Idea* (at least in part) and borrowed from it, also sees that the title of the poem corresponds to the central theme of Schopenhauer's work; he argues that it is a poem "about rebirth in terms of the contrast made by Schopenhauer between 'the thing itself,' which for him was the world as will, and 'ideas about the thing,' which of course belonged to the world as idea." But Adams is unable or unwilling to grant the poem's assumption that "the thing itself" is Stevens' more radical version of Schopenhauer's cosmic will, a natural world modeled on the human will. He maintains instead that the poem is concerned with "the living reality of our experience in the world, as distinguished from and opposed to the dead abstractions which are our ideas about it." "The thing itself," he notes, is "the actual concrete experience" of the speaker "coming back to life after having been withdrawn and torpid and comparatively dead; and this concrete experience is what the poem is finally intended to evoke."[9]

William V. Davis also ignores the implications of Stevens' "the Thing Itself" and assumes that the poem contradicts its title. He contends, "Instead of giving us 'the Thing Itself,' as the title promises, the poem seems rather to provide only 'Ideas abut the Thing,' ideas which never really get us to 'the Thing Itself,' but, finally, only to a something, an 'it,' which, at best, is only 'like,' and then only 'like / A new knowledge of reality'—which may or may not be what has been meant by 'the Thing Itself.'"[10] If, however, Stevens' "the Thing Itself" is something like Schopenhauer's thing-in-itself, the contradiction dissolves, since "the Thing Itself" is the whole external world as the manifestation of will, not simply the bird's cry, which is only a "part of the colossal sun."

When we look upon the forces of nature, Schopenhauer writes, "it will require no great effort of the imagination to recognise, even at so great a distance, our own nature." That which in us is conscious but in the "weakest of its manifestations, only strives blindly and dumbly in a one-sided and unchangeable manner, must yet in both cases come under the name of will, as it is everywhere one and the same—just as the first dim light of dawn must share the name of sunlight with the rays of the full mid-day" (*World* 1:153). This passage is included in a discussion of Schopenhauer in Arthur Kenyon Rogers' *A Student's History of Philosophy,* from which Stevens quotes in his lecture "A Collect of Philosophy." Rogers also quotes another passage from Schopenhauer that uses a figure—the morning dream versus reality—incorporated into "Not Ideas about the Thing." Schopenhauer is describing the man who has freed himself both from the illusion of the world as idea and from the craving of the will: "Life and its forms now pass before him as a fleeting illusion, as a light morning dream before half-waking eyes, the real world already shining through it so that it can no longer deceive." (*World* 1:505).[11] In Saunders' preface to *The Wisdom of Life* Stevens read: "The whole world . . . with all its phenomena of change, growth and development, is ultimately the manifestation of Will—*Wille und Vorstellung*—a blind force conscious of itself only when it reaches the stage of intellect. . . . [T]he will, the thing-in-itself—in philosophical language, the *noumenon*—always remains as the permanent element" (*Wisdom* x). If we read "Not Ideas about the Thing but the Thing Itself" as if it had absorbed Schopenhauer, the title is quite precise, since its motive is to privilege the thing-in-itself, the *noumenon,* and not the *phenomena* of "sleep's faded papier-mâché."

Whether or not Schopenhauer inhabits "Not Ideas about the Thing," he was clearly on Stevens' mind during the period when the poems of *The Rock* were composed. In November 1951, a few months before the composition of "Lebensweisheitspielerei," Stevens delivered "A Collect of Philosophy" at the University of Chicago. Its subject is the poetic nature of selected philosophic ideas, and Stevens gives a central place to Schopenhauer's world as will, which he calls an "eccentric philosophic apparatus on the grand scale" (*OP* 272). He quotes at length a summary of Schopenhauer's theory that includes the following:

> The eternally striving, energizing power which is working everywhere in the universe—in the instinct of the animal, the life process of the plant, the blind force of inorganic matter—what is this but the will that underlies all existence? . . . Reality, then, is will. . . . We must leave out of our conception of the universal will that action for intelligent ends which characterizes human willing. . . . The will is thus far deeper seated than the intellect; it is the blind man carrying on his shoulders the lame man who can see. (*OP* 274)

It would be instructive to read Stevens' own summary of Schopenhauer; unfortunately, he lifted this one from *A Student's History of Philosophy.*

It *is* instructive, however, to read Stevens' characterization of Schopenhauer's concept. He calls it "the text of a poem although not a happy one." It is, he says, "the cosmic poem of the ascent into heaven" (*OP* 274), a somewhat opaque description that perhaps alludes to the metaphysical or transcendent nature of Schopenhauer's theory and its ability to allow us to ascend beyond our human limitations. Earlier in the lecture he had clarified the concept of "the cosmic poem" in relation to another philosophical concept: "It is cosmic poetry because it makes us realize in the same way in which an escape from all our limitations would make us realize that we are creatures, not of a part, which is our every day limitation, but of a whole for which, for the most part, we have as yet no language." He adds, in a figure that recalls the conclusion of "Not Ideas about the Thing," "This sudden change of a lesser life for a greater one is like a change of winter for spring or any other transmutation of poetry" (*OP* 271).

Schopenhauer appears in the lecture in other guises as well. His theory is an example of a philosophy which is "no longer part of our thought and yet perpetuates itself," an "eccentric" conception that is nevertheless "not junk" (*OP* 279). He is also proposed as a possible example of a philosopher who experienced the "shortenings of mental processes that the poet experiences": "The whole scheme of the world as will may very well have occurred to Schopenhauer in an instant. The time he spent afterward in the explication of that instant is another matter" (*OP* 277). Although statements such as this, and the lecture as a whole, have the effect of blurring the distinction between the philosopher and the poet, I am not attempting to transform Stevens into a philosopher nor to reduce his poems to philosophical statements. I do want to suggest, however, that Schopenhauer's writings, and the two-part translation of *Aphorismen zur Lebensweisheit* in particular, may be usefully read as intertexts of *The Rock,* revealing the significance of elements and particulars otherwise invisible. This is the case, I believe, with "Lebensweisheitspielerei."

"Lebensweisheitspielerei" is a poem of indigence, as its poverty of language indicates. It speaks of the poor, the weak, the unaccomplished; it is as if the speaker, *as the poet,* were himself unaccomplished, without a command of language or an adequate imagination. This is the plain sense of things taken to another level. The poem suggests its poetic indigence through repetition; the poet has created a poem out of the fewest possible words, has eked out his meager supply of language:

> *Weaker* and *weaker,* the sunlight falls
> In *the* afternoon. *The* proud and *the* strong
> Have departed.

Those that *are* left *are* the unaccomplished,
The finally human,
Natives of a dwindled sphere.

Their *indigence is an indigence*
That *is an indigence* of the light,
A *stellar pallor* that hangs on the threads.

Little by *little* the poverty
Of autumnal space becomes
A look, *a* few words spoken.

Each person completely touches us
With what *he is* and as *he is,*
In the stale grandeur of annihilation.

As my italics indicate, this tactic reaches its culmination in the third stanza with the word *indigence* itself, the repetition of the verb, and the repeated notes of "stellar pallor," as if not only words but sounds were in short supply.

Against this poverty of form and sense of loss runs a seemingly contradictory strain of affirmation and perception. The unaccomplished, not the proud and the strong, are the "finally human." The autumnal poverty, reduced to "A look, a few words spoken," is revelatory, so that each person is uncovered "completely," touching us "With what he is and as he is." As in "The Plain Sense of Things," "A Quiet Normal Life," and "Final Soliloquy of the Interior Paramour," poverty, loss, bareness lead to a kind of clairvoyance. What remains unstated in these poems is the bond between the two states. Is the lack of imagination a necessary condition for insight here at the end? Is the indigence of old age a requisite state for seeing each person "as he is"? Is there a connection between the speaker's age and his plain sense of things? Schopenhauer argues in *Aphorismen zur Lebensweisheit* that this is indeed the case.

The last chapter of *Counsels and Maxims,* part two of Saunders' translation of *Aphorismen zur Lebensweisheit,* is titled (by the translator) "The Ages of Life," and it ends with Schopenhauer's discussion of the virtues of old age, foremost of which is the ability to see things as they are. This quality is attributed, as it is in the poems of *The Rock,* to old age's plain sense of things:

> It is only then that he sees things quite plain, and takes them for that which they really are: while in earlier years he saw a phantom-world, put together out of the whims and crotchets of his own mind, inherited prejudice and strange delusion: the real world was hidden from him, or the vision of it distorted. The first thing that experience finds to do is to free us from the phantoms of the brain—those false notions that have been put into us in youth. (*Counsels* 134)

In "The Plain Sense of Things" Stevens' implied figure for this experience of clarity, for seeing what lies behind the surface, is the network of bare tree limbs which had been obscured by summer foliage: "After the leaves have fallen, we return / To a plain sense of things." The foliage was more beautiful, and its loss is like "an end of the imagination," but what is revealed exposes the underlying structure. Schopenhauer's figure is similar in suggesting a contrast between outward beauty and inner workings:

> From the point of view we have been taking up until now, life may be compared to a piece of embroidery, of which, during the first half of his time, a man gets a sight of the right side, and during the second half, of the wrong. The wrong side is not so pretty as the right, but it is more instructive; it shows the way in which the threads have been worked together. (*Counsels* 135)

In "Lebensweisheitspielerei" what is seen plainly is not the natural but the human, although the principle of reduction seems to be the same as that of "The Plain Sense of Things." In the "autumnal space" of the poem—the "dwindled sphere" of old age—the deceptions of outward appearance have been discarded, and the "finally human" is revealed. It is in the "poverty" of age, another figure of reduction, that "Each person *completely* touches us / With what he is and as he is." It is not a question of seeing better but of seeing completely and exactly what the proud and the strong cannot see. Schopenhauer's figure for seeing each person "as he is" is the familiar one of removing the mask.

> Towards the close of life, much the same thing happens as at the end of a *bal masqué*—the masks are taken off. Then you can see who the people really are, with whom you have come into contact in your passage through the world. For by the end of life characters have come out in their true light . . . and all shams have fallen to pieces. (*Counsels* 151)

In this discussion Schopenhauer also anticipates Stevens' association of poverty with old age in several poems of *The Rock*. For Stevens, in these poems poverty is a figure for the decrease of life at the end, what is left after the affluence of youth has been spent. It is "with health as with money," Schopenhauer says. In old age, "our position is like that of the investor who begins to entrench upon his capital." He "feels himself growing poorer and poorer," and his "fall from wealth to poverty becomes faster every moment . . . until at last he has absolutely nothing left" (*Counsels* 141–42). Yet "It is poverty's speech that seeks us out the most," Stevens writes in "To an Old Philosopher in Rome." Both he and Schopenhauer recognize the paradox of a poverty that is at the same time a source of grandeur and insight. The paradox is contained in some of the mixed figures in the poems of *The Rock*—the "Profound poetry of the poor and of the dead" and the "afflatus of ruin" of "To an Old Philosopher," the "stale grandeur of annihilation" of "Lebensweisheitspielerei," the "thought" in which "we collect ourselves" in "Final Soliloquy of the Interior Paramour," which is figured as "a single shawl / Wrapped tightly round us, since we are poor."

For Schopenhauer the poverty of old age is welcomed as a path to the only permanent escape from suffering that he recognizes, which is a renunciation of the will. Since all suffering arises from the constant desire of the will, which can never be satisfied, the only happiness is to deny the will: "So long as we are the subject of willing, we can never have lasting happiness nor peace":

> But when some external cause or inward disposition lifts us suddenly out of the endless stream of willing, delivers knowledge from the slavery of the will, the attention is no longer directed to the motives of willing, but comprehends things free from their relation to the will, and thus observes them without personal interest, without subjectivity, purely objectively, gives itself entirely up to them so far as they are ideas, but not in so far as they are motives. Then all at once the peace which we were seeking . . . comes to us of its own accord, and it is well with us. (*World* 1:254)

The artist may achieve this state momentarily, but the only permanent peace is found in the relinquishment of the will. One way to do this is through a deliberate asceticism, but "most men only attain to it" by "suffering in general, as it is inflicted by fate. . . . often only at the approach of death" (*World* 1:506–7). Curiously, then, for Schopenhauer, the only escape from the suffering of life is achieved by suffering itself:

> What really gives its wonderful and ambiguous character to our life is this, that two diametrically opposite aims constantly cross each other in it; that of the individual will directed to chimerical happiness in an ephemeral, dream-like, and delusive existence, in which, with reference to the past, happiness and unhappiness are a matter of indifference, and the present is every moment becoming the past; and that of fate visibly enough directed to the destruction of our happiness, and thereby to the mortification of our will and the abolition of the illusion that holds us chained in the bonds of this world. (*World* 3:466)

Like Stevens in *The Rock*, Schopenhauer recognizes the paradoxical relation between the poverty, weakness, and misery of the approach to death and its liberation from the illusions of "the strong and the proud." He notes that "fate and the course of things care for us better than we ourselves ... and meet us everywhere with healing sorrow, the panacea of our misery" (*World* 3:466).

In *The Wisdom of Life* Schopenhauer remarks on one other quality of old age that Stevens incorporates into *The Rock*. It is then, he says, that the man of achievement, the artist, the musician, the philosopher, may properly appreciate his fame. While "fame and youth are too much for a mortal at one and the same time," when youth has departed there is great consolation in looking back on works that have survived. Schopenhauer uses a figure for fame that readers familiar with Stevens' poem "The Green Plant" will recognize:

> Youth has enough and to spare in itself, and must rest content with what it has. But when the delights and joys of life fall away in old age, as the leaves from a tree in autumn, fame buds forth opportunely, like a plant that is green in winter. Fame is, as it were, the fruit that must grow all the summer before it can be enjoyed at Yule. There is no greater consolation in age than the feeling of having put the whole force of one's youth into works which still remain young. (*Wisdom* 131–32)

"The Green Plant" (*CP* 506), which was first published in a group with "Lebensweisheitspielerei" and "The Plain Sense of Things" among others, has most often been read as a poem about a reality that resists the transformations of the imagination. The green plant is set in opposition to the colors of autumn, which represent a "constant secondariness, / A turning down toward finality." They are "falsifications from a sun / In a mirror, without heat," and "the shadows of the trees / Are like wrecked umbrellas." The green plant, Helen Regueiro argues, is "a persistence of reality in spite of the shadows and the dimming sun." In its refusal to be mastered, it asserts "the existence of a reality outside the realm of the imagination."[12] It is certainly true that the green plant is associated with reality in the poem, and that in *The Rock* reality generally refuses to be mastered, but the Schopenhauer intertext raises the possibility that the figure carries further significance. It appears that "The Green Plant" is yet another poem in which Stevens looks back over his career, although this dimension of the poem is deeply buried. It also appears to be a companion poem to "The Planet on the Table," which is more explicit about the practice of assessing one's fame.

"The Green Plant" begins with a description of the coming of autumn reminiscent of "an end of the imagination" in the opening of "The Plain Sense of Things":

> Silence is a shape that has passed.
> Otu-bre's lion-roses have turned to paper
> And the shadows of the trees
> Are like wrecked umbrellas.
>
> The effete vocabulary of summer
> No longer says anything.

Regueiro's focus is on the artificiality of this description: "The organic process has given way to mechanical images: paper, wrecked umbrellas, shadows of trees." She notes that "even the forest is a painted forest ('the maroon and olive forest'), a legendary place."[13] The poem indeed refers to "the legend of the maroon and olive forest," not to indicate that it is painted, however, but to suggest that it has become a story from the past. Like everything else in the poem save one, it is diminished. The poem sees the end of the year as the wreck of summer, "a constant secondariness, / A turning down toward finality." Everything is a shadow of its summer self:

> Except that a green plant glares, as you look
> At the legend of the maroon and olive forest,
> Glares, outside of the legend, with the barbarous green
> Of the harsh reality of which it is part.

Regueiro wishes to make the green plant an emblem of reality itself, and on first reading this appears to be the case. It is "outside of the legend" that the other plants of summer have become; its barbarous

green is associated with "the harsh reality of which it is part." Yet the
final phrase recalls the last line of "The Planet on the Table" (*CP*
532), in which the same phrasing is used to refer not to reality but
to Stevens' own poems:

> What mattered was that they should bear
> Some lineament or character,
>
> Some affluence, if only half-perceived,
> In the poverty of their words,
> Of the planet of which they were part.

In both poems the poet is at the end looking back; in both the lan-
guage of poetry is in question—effete in one, poor in the other. In
both, "Other makings of the sun / Were waste and welter," and in
both the central figure—the green plant, the book of collected
poems which is the planet on the table—has alone survived the
"turning down toward finality." When, in "The Green Plant,"
Stevens has the plant glaring "outside of the legend," he is suggest-
ing obliquely what he says outright in "The Planet on the Table." He
was "glad he had written his poems." Like Dylan Thomas, he denies
he has written them for fame. Modestly, he notes, "They were of a
remembered time / Or of something seen that he liked." What mat-
ters most in both poems is that "they should bear / Some lineament
or character" of the reality "of which they were part." His modesty
does not, however, erase the satisfaction he feels in both poems in
looking back at them, and Schopenhauer's figure is not ineffective
as a description of the tone of both: "when the delights and joys of
life fall away in old age, as the leaves from a tree in autumn, fame
buds forth opportunely, like a plant that is green in winter."

Stevens' title "The Planet on the Table" brings us back to the two
worlds of *The Rock*, which here coalesce:

> His self and the sun were one
> And his poems, although makings of his self,
> Were no less makings of the sun.

Among the possible interpretations of these lines is one not inconsistent with Schopenhauer's concept that the world is at the same time "entirely idea," the product of a "knowing subject," and entirely will, "the side of its inmost nature—its kernel—the thing-in-itself" (*World* 1:38–39). "That which in us pursues its ends by the light of knowledge," Schopenhauer writes, and that which in nature "only strives blindly and dumbly," must "in both cases come under the name of Will, as it is everywhere one and the same." He concludes that "the name *will* denotes that which is the inner nature of everything in the world, and the one kernel of every phenomenon" (*World* 1:153). The extent to which the two worlds of *The Rock* have absorbed Schopenhauer's two worlds of will and idea is difficult to determine; the question of the relation between any two texts is a vexed one, troubling but fruitful as a method of reading. Certainly, Stevens' larger world is both more whimsical and more benevolent than Schopenhauer's world as insatiable will, but it shares with Schopenhauer's concept the notion that the inner world of the self is a part of a larger world that resembles the self, so that one is, like Stevens' portrait of the dying Santayana (and of himself at the end), "part both in the inch and in the mile."

3 / Penelope, Mr. Homburg, and the Interior Paramour

Whether one arrives at the idea of God as a philosopher or as a poet matters greatly.
—STEVENS, "A Collect of Philosophy"

IN 1950 STEVENS CONTEMPLATED a long poem on God and the imagination. If he had completed the project, it is quite likely that we would now read the poems of *The Rock* differently, much as the reflections of "Notes toward a Supreme Fiction" modified our reading of the poems of the previous decade. As it happened, he completed only the opening lines, which he titled "Final Soliloquy of the Interior Paramour" and sent to Joseph Bennett, editor of the *Hudson Review.* He told Bennett, "I had originally intended to write a long poem on the subject of the present poem but got no farther than the statement that God and the imagination are one. The implications of this statement were to follow, and may still" (*Letters* 701). "The implications never followed," Lucy Beckett writes,[1] but some of them did in fact follow in later poems of *The Rock* and after, particularly in poems such as "The World as Meditation" and "Looking across the Fields and Watching the Birds Fly," which treat the subject directly. Some of them are intimated in "Final Soliloquy of the Interior Paramour" itself, although masked by an enigmatic language that has allowed readers to interpret the proposition in the most conventional sense.

Although only a fragment of a poem he never wrote, "Final

Soliloquy of the Interior Paramour" (*CP* 524) obviously held some significance for Stevens, and he chose it as the concluding poem—his own final soliloquy—of *Selected Poems,* published in England by Faber and Faber in 1953. He wrote to Herbert Weinstock of Knopf that "this is an extremely good poem with which to wind up the English book" (*Letters* 734). It is the only poem of what would become *The Rock* included in *Selected Poems*—most of those poems had not been completed at the time Stevens made his selection. Its tone of finality and its placement toward the end of *The Rock* are thus somewhat deceptive, in that it was apparently one of the earliest poems to be composed, establishing the direction for those to follow and contributing the line that underlies so much of the late poetry—"We say God and the imagination are one." Stevens' remarks to Joseph Bennett indicate that this was, for him, the central concept of the poem, and I want to begin with this formulation and the readings it has generated. But I also want to pursue some of its implications, attempting what Stevens had projected for himself in the long poem never written.

Taken out of its context in "Final Soliloquy," the line would appear to be merely another of Stevens' glorifications of the imagination—the human imagination as God—and overwhelmingly readers have interpreted it as some variation of this construction. For Anthony Whiting the poem is a reaffirmation of "the power of the imagination to create the 'supreme fictions,' the fictive constructs that are the world in which we dwell." Richard Blessing writes that it is "our fiction, our imagined meaning" that constitutes the poem's "unifying force," its "'single shawl' which we wrap around ourselves against the cold." Edward Kessler reads the equating of God with the imagination as indicating that Stevens' "faith is a faith in himself," while Ronald Sukenick, who reads "Final Soliloquy" as a poem about "the power of the imagination," concludes, "The point of the identification of God and the imagination is to give an idea of the magnitude of this experience by connecting it with a traditional one." Denis Donoghue alters the line, adding *human,* to make his point that in the tradition of American poetry to which Stevens belongs, "the only way to heal the breach between God, nature, and man is by becoming God and rearranging things according to your own 'light.' . . . Hence we say, God and the human imagination are one. The saint is the man of thought."[2]

Donoghue's alteration makes explicit what is assumed in all these readings: that the imagination alluded to is the *human* imagination, and that Stevens is elevating the human imagination to the level of God. If he had wished to say that, however, the line would have been more properly phrased as "We say the imagination and God are one." It is instead expressed as a statement about God. Against its usual interpretation, Janet McCann rightly observes that "it might as readily be taken to mean what it says: that God *is* imagination."[3] That is what it literally says and that appears to be the explication Stevens gives it in his own gloss: "Proposita: 1. God and the imagination are one. 2. The thing imagined is the imaginer. The second equals the thing imagined and the imaginer are one. Hence, I suppose, the imaginer is God" ("Adagia," *OP* 202). Here Stevens restates his thesis by substituting "the thing imagined" for God and "the imaginer" for the imagination; he concludes that God is not simply the thing imagined, the assumption of his poetry almost to the end, but that God is in fact the imaginer, the assumption of many of the last poems. And if we read the line in the way that Stevens does here—that God is the imaginer, the agent and not the object of the imagination—the poem as a whole says something quite different from its customary interpretation.

It begins, as do so many of the *Rock* poems, in an atmosphere in which poverty and weakness lead to transcendence:

> Light the first light of evening, as in a room
> In which we rest and, for small reason, think
> The world imagined is the ultimate good.
>
> This is, therefore, the intensest rendezvous.
> It is in that thought that we collect ourselves,
> Out of all the indifferences, into one thing:
>
> Within a single thing, a single shawl
> Wrapped tightly round us, since we are poor, a warmth,
> A light, a power, the miraculous influence.

If God is the *source* of imagination in the poem and if the speaker and his world are that which is imagined, then the meaning of the third line shifts dramatically. "The world imagined" is not the world of the speaker's imagination—in his weakness he seems incapable of imagining a world. It is the world conceived, "for small reason," as God's imagination. ("The world imagined" preserves the ambiguity of agency, as is so often the case when Stevens speaks of imagination in *The Rock*.) Irrationally, illogically, the speaker finds comfort in thinking of himself as residing within the mind of God, and he recognizes in his hyperbole the extremity of his conception. It is the "ultimate good," the "intensest rendezvous," and, one might argue, the supreme fiction. It is the one "thought"—the world is imagined by God—that offers protection in a setting that is otherwise dark, cold, poor, and indifferent. The frailty of such a belief, the recognition that it is without basis, no more than a fiction, is conveyed by Stevens' image of the thought as "a single shawl / Wrapped tightly round us, since we are poor." A shawl is a humble, seemingly inadequate form of protection, one associated with old age and infirmity, but here it is "a warmth, / A light, a power, the miraculous influence."

"Miraculous" would be an extravagant term if the poem were not in fact suggesting a moment of transcendence, the speaker's sense of being in touch with God by means of what is no more than a thought, a fiction. Interestingly, each time he approaches his conception of God and the imagination Stevens' speaker backs away from the enormity of what he is saying by qualifying it. He does not say that the world imagined is the ultimate good, only that he *thinks* so, for small reason; nor does he claim God and the imagination are one, only that he *says* so, again presumably for small reason. These qualified assertions are in keeping with the speaker's own sense of weakness and imaginative poverty. He is in the curious position of wishing to introduce a daring supposition about the nature of reality without taking credit for it. Like the speaker of "A Quiet Normal Life" (*CP* 523), the poem that immediately precedes "Final Soliloquy" in *The Rock* and is another version of it, he wishes to convey the impression that "His place, as he sat and as he thought, was not / In anything that he constructed."

It is thus curious that "Final Soliloquy" has so often been read as a poem about the power of the human imagination, the elevation of the self to God-like status. As is the case with all of the late poetry, the endeavor of the poem is in the opposite direction, effacing the individual imagination or mind as a mere "inhabitant" (to revert again to the language of the preceding poem) of a larger imagination, a "central mind." However obscurely, the speaker senses an "order" or "knowledge" within which he rests, and he attributes to this larger self, not his own best-forgotten self, the volition which "arranged the rendezvous":

> Here, now, we forget each other and ourselves.
> We feel the obscurity of an order, a whole,
> A knowledge, that which arranged the rendezvous,
>
> Within its vital boundary, in the mind.
> We say God and the imagination are one . . .
> How high that highest candle lights the dark.
>
> Out of this same light, out of the central mind,
> We make a dwelling in the evening air,
> In which being there together is enough.

Line fifteen had originally read "How high that highest candle lights the world!" but before publication in the *Hudson Review* Stevens thought better of it, removed the exclamation point, and changed *world* to *dark* (*Letters* 701). Although the changes make it a better line, the original version would have clarified the relationship between this passage and the first stanza, in which the actual lighting of a candle leads to the thought that "The world imagined is the ultimate good." In the fifth stanza the conception of God as the imagination is the metaphorical "highest candle" and provides the light in which the speaker makes a "dwelling." Harold Bloom, missing the point of Stevens' candle metaphor, asks, "How high does any single candle, even the highest, light the dark? Stevens is not being ironic, but the passage, and the poem, assert less than they seem to assert."[4] On the contrary, if Stevens' intimations about

God and the imagination are disclosed, the passage and the poem assert more than has previously been thought.

Bloom's reading also brings up another vexing question, or at least one that has provoked readers' speculations, and that is the identity of the "Interior Paramour" of the title, which in turn leads to questions about the poem's speaker. Some readers have followed Bloom in labeling the paramour as the muse, and Bloom explicates the title by suggesting that it may imply "not that the muse is about to perish but that poet and muse are about to be so joined that every remaining poem will be a dialogue of one," which must mean that this poem is spoken by the muse. While resisting the notion that she is a traditional muse, Barbara Fisher concurs that it is the muse who speaks: "Perhaps for the first time, in this very late poem, we are permitted to hear the poet's interior voice directly." Adalaide Kirby Morris identifies Stevens' paramour as a "personified abstraction" of "the muse of imagination," and Joseph Carroll calls her "the ancient mother," the "medium and symbol" of Stevens' visionary power. Jacqueline Brogan and Mary Arensberg emphasize her presence as a feminine muse-like figure within Stevens' male authorial voice. Brogan finds that the poem depicts "the recognition and recovery of the feminine voice" in late Stevens. The word "paramour" suggest a "romance" and "intimacy" in the poem that is dependent on sexual difference. As she argues, "The most telling sign of this is the plural pronoun 'we' and that most feminine of articles, the 'shawl.'" Arensberg appropriates the appellation "interior paramour" to name the feminine presence in Stevens' canon as a whole, writing that "Stevens' interior paramour is present from the beginning, not as reality but as a reflection of the movements of her poet's mind and as their exciting cause. For she is Stevens' metaphor for the extra-linguistic source of poetry and a trope of imaginative desire, a 'fiction that results from feeling,' that conceals the vacancy from which she rises." "Final Soliloquy" is "an attempt to actually name her," and the "intensest rendezvous" of the poem is a "metaphoric coupling" of "lover-poet and muse-paramour."[5]

The assumptions behind all these readings is that the paramour must be feminine and that she is "interior" because she resides within the poet. "The literary muse, conventionally summoned from above and beyond, represents inspiration that strikes from without; she is external to the poet," Barbara Fisher writes. "In contrast, the paramour is an inner presence."[6] Both these assumptions—that the paramour is feminine and that she resides inside the poet—are, I believe, mistaken, although quite understandable, and they have skewed readings of the poem, especially in regard to the poem's speaker. *Paramour* is a notably interesting word in the context of the poem since, according to the *Oxford English Dictionary*, it may have originated as a shortened form of "for love of God." In devotional language, it was used to refer to the Virgin Mary, Jesus Christ, or God, and in sexual language it was and is more apt to be used to refer to the person beloved than to the lover. That is, the paramour is most often the recipient of love, and the term need not be feminine, since it is used to refer to a beloved of either sex.

Stevens' title indicates that the poem we are reading is the soliloquy of the interior paramour, which creates something of a problem with the customary readings, since they identify the paramour with the feminine muse or some related feminine figure. These assumptions lead Thomas Grey, for example, to the conclusion that Stevens here "speaks in the voice of a female, no longer the silently inspiring muse, who has actually at last absorbed her poet." The voice of this poem, however, sounds no different from the voice of the surrounding poems. It is clearly the aged, "poor," diminished persona whose voice pervades *The Rock* who speaks here as well— a persona whose circumstances and voice reflect those of the poet. Readers have tried to evade this problem through various strategies—"she speaks through the poet" (Carroll), or "the voice . . . is that of the poet's 'we,' composed of his fictionalized self, the major man, and his feminine double and mate" (Arensberg)[7]—but they are unconvincing. What has not been recognized is that the Stevens-persona who speaks throughout *The Rock* is himself the interior paramour, who, it turns out, is not in fact a feminine figure in spite of universal assumptions to the contrary.

It is perhaps the word *interior* that has led to the confusion. Why would the lover be described as an *interior* paramour if she or he did not reside within the poet? In what other sense could a paramour be thought of as *interior*? The answer lies relatively close to the surface in the poem's binary of interiority and exteriority, and it is necessary to note carefully what is enclosed, contained within, and what constitutes the container. This spatial pattern runs throughout the poem. In the first stanza the speaker thinks, for small reason, "The world imagined is the ultimate good," and it is "in that thought" that he collects himself "Out of all the indifferences into one thing." This is repeated with a slightly different emphasis to underscore the sense of being contained within some larger order. "Within a single thing," he begins, finding a figure adequate to his sense of being the thing contained: "a single shawl / Wrapped tightly round us, since we are poor." It is within this enclosure that he feels, obscurely, "an order, a whole, / A knowledge, that which arranged the rendezvous, / Within its vital boundary, in the mind." This last line is especially revealing, since the speaker identifies the container within whose boundary he is contained as something apart from himself.[8] It is at this point that he says, "God and the imagination are one," linking God as imagination with the "mind," "knowledge," "whole," and "order" of the preceding lines as well as the "central mind" of the last stanza.

The imagery shifts at the poem's conclusion, but it continues its spatial dimension. The concept that God is the imaginer has become the "highest candle" that "lights the dark," and it is "Out of this same light, out of the central mind" that the speaker makes a "dwelling," "In which being there together is enough." The poem begins with the speaker enclosed within a "single shawl," a figure for his thought that "The world imagined is the ultimate good," and ends with him enclosed within a "dwelling," a figure for his thought that "God and the imagination are one." (In the preceding poem, "A Quiet Normal Life," he is an "inhabitant" of a place not of his own construction.) It is the speaker's interiority that is made emphatic throughout "Final Soliloquy," and it is the speaker who takes comfort in the thought that he is the paramour, the recipient of "a warmth, / A light, a power, the miraculous influence" of "that which arranged the rendezvous." He is not the active partner in this rendezvous, the arranger, the lover; he is the beloved. His mind does not contain or imagine the world; he is contained within the world's imagination, the imagination of a "central mind." It is this extraordinary conception, inscribed ambiguously not only in "Final Soliloquy of the Interior Paramour" but in *The Rock* as a whole, that has impeded readings of the last poems and especially of this one, which appears to wish both to disclose and to conceal the most eccentric and whimsical of all Stevens' fictions.

There is one word in the title that perhaps indicates Stevens' wish to disclose it. The poem is the *final* soliloquy of the interior paramour—a term that has appeared particularly puzzling. What is final about the soliloquy that becomes the poem? It has been taken to mean that the interior paramour, however interpreted, will no longer appear to the poet, that is, "final" as coming at the end. "The final appearance of the interior paramour argues an end to the unfulfilled desire which created the need for that paramour," Charles Berger writes. Bloom gives "final" a more positive reading—it is the muse's final *soliloquy,* in that remaining poems will be dialogues of the integrated muse and poet—but also takes it to mean coming at the end. That sense of finality is certainly present in many of the poems of *The Rock,* as here; but "final" has another, perhaps more relevant, meaning, which Mary Arensberg comes close to in her discussion of the interior paramour. Although I believe she is mistaken in her characterization of the paramour in the poem, she catches something of the nuance of "final" when she writes that the poem "is an attempt to actually name her. . . . Now, in the 'final soliloquy' we come to know her by name."[9] "Final" may also carry the sense of conclusive or definitive, as in "final cause" or "final purpose," or ultimate, as in "the ultimate good," the final good, of the poem's third line. Stevens often uses the term to suggest ultimate or conclusive; there are, among many other examples, the "thing final in itself and, therefore good" and the "final good" of "Notes toward a Supreme Fiction" (*CP* 405) and the "final simplification" of "Life on a Battleship" (*OP* 107). The paramour's soliloquy is final in that the poet says flatly and conclusively what before has been evasive—God and the imagination are one, the ultimate statement of the final fiction. It may at first appear ironic, then, that readers for the most part have been resistant to the fiction of the poem, preferring to interpret it as a conventional poem about the power of the human imagination, but the poet must bear some of the blame for that, holding back from the finality of his soliloquy and never completing the longer version that might have made it final.

Or perhaps not. Stevens' attempts at amplification usually led to further conjecture and speculation, and I am mindful of the lack of finality in my own reading of the poem, which runs counter to almost everything written about it. I would be less confident of my interpretation were it not supported by surrounding poems of *The Rock,* particularly by "The World as Meditation" and "Looking across the Fields and Watching the Birds Fly," two poems published together in 1952[10] that I want to read in conjunction with "Final Soliloquy." The fact that "The World as Meditation" could have served satisfactorily as the title for any of the three suggests the degree to which they are related.

"The World as Meditation" (*CP* 520) is one of only a handful of Stevens' poems that begin with an epigraph, and George Lensing, who has examined Stevens' epigraphs in *Wallace Stevens: A Poet's Growth,* notes that on the rare occasion when he does append one, he is offering it as "the lens through which . . . to view the poem." Lensing also observes that the sources of Stevens' epigraphs are not usually classical texts but popular works or journalistic articles, and this is indeed the case with "The World as Meditation." Its epigraph comes from the Romanian musician and composer Georges Enesco, and its source, Lensing has found, is a series of twenty conversations with Enesco that were broadcast in France in 1951, the year before the poem was published. Lensing speculates that Stevens saw a transcription of these broadcasts, since they were published (as *Les Souvenirs de Georges Enesco*) in 1955, after the poem's composition. What is telling about Stevens' epigraph is its divergence from Enesco's published words. "Stevens' transcription

of Enesco's words is not precise," Lensing writes,[11] and his impreci-
sion discloses one motif of the poem that has not been sufficiently
acknowledged.

In Stevens' epigraph Enesco says, "J'ai passé trop de temps à tra-
vailler mon violon, à voyager. Mais l'exercice essentiel du composi-
teur—la méditation—rien ne l'a jamais suspendu en moi. . . . Je vis
un rêve permanent, qui ne s'arrête ni nuit ni jour." (I have spent too
much time playing my violin and traveling. But the essential exer-
cise of the composer—meditation—nothing has ever kept me from
that. I live a permanent dream which does not cease, night or day.)
Lensing points out that this differs from Enesco's published text in
three respects. Enesco does not say exactly that his violin and travel
have taken "trop de temps," nor that meditation is the "exercice
essentiel du compositeur," but he says something quite similar. It is
the third variation that is most striking. Stevens alters Enesco's "je
porte en moi un rêve permanent; quelque chose frémit dans mon
coeur, qui ne s'arrête ni nuit, ni jour" to "Je vis un rêve permanent,
qui ne s'arrête ni nuit ni jour." "I carry within me a permanent
dream; something vibrates within my heart which does not cease
night or day" becomes "I live a permanent dream which does not
cease night or day." Lensing finds that the effect of the change "is to
make the habitual and constant dream more intrinsic, something to
be lived rather than taken up."[12] That is correct as far as it goes, but
the more significant result of the change is to create the same sense
of duality or ambiguity that is established in the title, "The World
as Meditation." It is the same equivocation to be found in "The
world imagined is the ultimate good" of "Final Soliloquy," which
obscures the identity of the imaginer, and in the uncertainty of
agency in the use of the word *imagination* in "The Plain Sense of
Things" (*CP* 502), where "the absence of the imagination had / Itself
to be imagined." "Je vis un rêve permanent, qui ne s'arrête ni nuit
ni jour" as an epigraph for a poem titled "The World as Meditation"
(*CP* 520) raises a question of interpretation—both for itself and for
its title—that "je *porte en moi* un rêve permanent" does not.

The question that it raises is the question that the poem as a
whole raises: whose dream, whose meditation is this, and what is its

nature? Does the title refer to the world as Penelope's meditation, as has been generally assumed, or is it "an inhuman meditation, larger than her own"? She meditates on the return of Ulysses: "But was it Ulysses? Or was it only the warmth of the sun / On her pillow?" In fact, the poem begins with a question:

Is it Ulysses that approaches from the east,
The interminable adventurer? The trees are mended.
That winter is washed away. Someone is moving

On the horizon and lifting himself up above it.
A form of fire approaches the cretonnes of Penelope,
Whose mere savage presence awakens the world in which
 she dwells.

Readers have remarked on the poem's ambiguity—"an example of Stevens' essentially ambiguous use of images," Doggett writes[13]— but the duality of the imagery is not an instance of an unresolvable ambiguity, since almost every quality ascribed to Ulysses more properly applies to the sun, which is not mentioned until near the poem's conclusion. It approaches from the east,[14] mends the trees, washes away winter, lifts itself above the horizon as a "form of fire" and a "savage presence" that "awakens the world." The question that the poem raises in its first line—is it Ulysses who approaches?—is answered in the negative almost from the beginning. No, it is not Ulysses, the poem suggests even in its opening stanzas; it is the spring sun. And this point is made more explicit as the poem progresses.

The more difficult question concerns the significance of this confusion between Ulysses and the sun. What does it mean that what is first taken to be the returning Ulysses turns out to be the sun? What qualities or values do Ulysses and Penelope represent, and what drama do they enact? A history of readings of the poem does not furnish confident answers, although there is some unanimity of opinion on Penelope and her relationship to the poet. Readers have generally admired the poem—Randall Jarrell, Harold

Bloom, Lucy Beckett, and George Lensing, among many others, have considered it as ranking among Stevens' best—but they have had difficulty with some of the poem's tropes, and particularly with the figure of Ulysses. Both William Burney and Mary Arensberg believe that he is Stevens' representative in the poem. Burney says that Stevens "identifies with Ulysses," and Arensberg more intricately argues that the "fiction of the muse displaces here the primacy of the poet's consciousness, and as their roles transpose, the mind of Stevens is frozen and contextualized into the myth of the 'interminable wanderer.'" Ulysses has also been seen by Richard Blessing as representing "that world of physical phenomena from which we are hopelessly separated" and by Mark Halliday as occupying the position of the reader: "Stevens, in his relation to the reader, thus resembles his Penelope in her relation to Ulysses." Loren Rusk, who initially associates Ulysses with a "realization of otherness," also testifies to the elusiveness of his identity and finds that by the end of the poem he has become the "Interior Paramour." "The reason . . . that Ulysses cannot be pinned down," she writes, "is that he has to do with the process of desire and striving that is being."[15]

There is much more agreement about Penelope's function in the poem, and she has customarily been identified either with the poet (or poetic imagination) or the muse. Bloom has it both ways, noting that "the never-satisfied mind of Penelope is analogous to the mind of Stevens" but also that "Penelope ends as Stevens' finest vision of his muse." She is also the muse for Arensberg, as well as "a counterpart of the poet" for Rusk, the imagination for Halliday, and Stevens himself for Frank Lentricchia. In *Wallace Stevens and the Seasons*, Lensing enumerates the parallels between Stevens and Penelope:

> As a poem about a separated husband and wife, "The World as Meditation" cannot be read without reference to Stevens and his own wife. Here, with remarkable skill, Stevens insinuates his own loneliness into that of a woman. They share other things in common: Penelope's art of weaving is not unlike the labor of the

poet. . . . Penelope's anguish is Stevens' anguish, just as her compensation through meditation is also his. It is this fact that accounts for the poem's underlying emotional pathos. Penelope's "barbarous strength" is the source of Stevens' own role in writing this poem and others.[16]

Whether or not Stevens saw his marital situation in the story of Penelope and Ulysses, as Lensing speculates, there seems to me little doubt that Penelope and not Ulysses is his representative in the poem, although not necessarily as the poet, the muse, or the poetic imagination. This leap is easily made—if Penelope is Stevens' spokeswoman, then the poem must be about the poet's meditation on the world, the world as the poet's meditation. It is that, among other things, but to limit it to a conventional and habitual reading (another Stevens poem about the power of the poetic imagination) is to overlook the more challenging intimations of its epigraph and title.

Voicing the conventional reading of the title, Frank Lentricchia states that Penelope is "the single artificer of the world in which she dwells, the principle of high formalist imagination," and that "the world as meditation is wholly hers." Voicing the conventional reading of the epigraph, Barbara Fisher states that "Penelope is clearly *compositeur* of the world she contemplates, the dreamer of the 'rêve permanent, qui ne s'arrête ni nuit ne jour.'" But it is not clear that Penelope is the composer of the world she contemplates, and it is not obviously true that the world as meditation is wholly hers. The assumptions of Lentricchia and Fisher, which mirror the majority opinion of the many readings "The World as Meditation" has received, are not wholly wrong, but they are inadequate as accounts of the poem. It is true that Penelope is a composer, but what she composes is a self to meet the self of Ulysses, which she also imagines:

> She has composed, so long, a self with which to welcome him,
> Companion to his self for her, which she imagined,
> Two in a deep-founded sheltering, friend and dear friend.

Lensing notes accurately of this passage, "This self-composition is an act of the imagination—here not so much world as meditation as self as meditation."[17] What Penelope does *not* compose is the world as meditation of the title, the world of the sun. Although there are two meditations in the poem, human and inhuman, the endeavor of the poem is in fact to correct the notion that what approaches from the east is a product of the human imagination, the Ulysses Penelope imagines. The movement is the same as that in "Not Ideas about the Thing but the Thing Itself" (*CP* 534), in which the speaker, awakening like Penelope at dawn, hears a bird's cry that initially "Seemed like a sound in his mind," but eventually is recognized as something external to himself and his imagination; it is instead a "part of the colossal sun." "The World as Meditation" asks a similar question of Penelope: was it her meditation that she experiences as a "savage presence," or was it something larger, though similar?

> But was it Ulysses? Or was it only the warmth of the sun
> On her pillow? The thought kept beating in her like her heart.
> The two kept beating together. It was only day.

It was not Ulysses, *her* meditation; it was only day. The *only* of "only the warmth of the sun" and "only day" is somewhat ironic (like the *mere* of "mere savage presence") in view of the extraordinary claims the poem makes about the sun and the coming of day—that they are a part of a second meditation described in the poem, the world as meditation of the title.

Penelope's awareness of this second and parallel meditation is the "thought [that] kept beating in her like her heart." She had first sensed it as the beloved sensing the approach of her lover in the opening stanzas and now, in their meeting in the concluding stanzas, she senses it as a "dear friend":

> It was Ulysses and it was not. Yet they had met,
> Friend and dear friend and a planet's encouragement.
> The barbarous strength within her would never fail.

Although many readers find the conclusion of the poem inconclusive, there *is* a consummation here of an unexpected kind. The warmth Penelope experiences is not the presence of Ulysses but the warmth of "Final Soliloquy"—"a warmth, / A light, a power, the miraculous influence." As in "Notes toward a Supreme Fiction," *warmth* also carries a sexual undertone, a "warmth . . . for lovers at last accomplishing / Their love" (*CP* 391). It is the warmth of the sun as Ulysses—"It was Ulysses and it was not"—the sun, "a planet's encouragement," as "Friend and dear friend," the sun conceived in the place of the lover. This is the meaning of the sun-Ulysses parallels that run throughout the poem. It is not that Ulysses is like the sun, but that the sun—and the world as meditation that it represents—is now seen as fulfilling the role of Ulysses as wanderer (interminably approaching from the east) and companion ("Friend and dear friend"). The "barbarous strength" now within her that "would never fail" is her response to the sun's "savage presence," and this strength is suggested by the serenity she exhibits in the poem's final stanza (which is often misread to mean the opposite, the failure of consummation). The thought that beats in her like her heart is that the world she inhabits, the coming of spring she senses, is itself a part of a larger meditation of which she is not the subject but the object: "The trees had been mended, as an essential exercise / In an inhuman meditation, larger than her own." This is the element of the poem its commentators have been unable to read, and it is the element that links Penelope to the persona of "Final Soliloquy of the Interior Paramour."

Loren Rusk has argued that Ulysses ultimately becomes the "Interior Paramour" of "The World as Meditation," but it seems to me that Penelope occupies that position in the same manner as does the speaker of "Final Soliloquy"—the paramour as the beloved, the object of love and not the lover. Several readers have sensed such a perspective in the poem without recognizing its implications. "It is the ultimate abstraction of the lover seeking the beloved," Frank Doggett maintains, "in this poem depicted from the point of view of the woman or of the longing of the object to be reached by the subject." C. Roland Wagner echoes Doggett, noting that Stevens switches the perspective from the more common "longing of the subject to reach an unattainable object." "Penelope *seems* to be an unmoved mover in the world she contemplates," Barbara Fisher comments. "But she is herself a 'point of vision and desire' and may be understood as a projection of her husband's intense wish to return home."[18] Penelope is in truth a "point of vision and desire" (the phrase is from "An Ordinary Evening in New Haven"), but the function of this perspective is not, I think, a projection of Ulysses' desire to return to her, which would make it a very different poem indeed. It is rather to allow Penelope to reach the same insight reached by the persona of "Final Soliloquy," of which "The World as Meditation" is to some extent a rewriting. What Penelope comes to understand is what is concluded in the earlier poem—that in her emotional poverty and need (which parallels the poverty of "Final Soliloquy") she experiences the "intensest rendezvous" in a "thought" (both poems turn on this "thought"), that the "world imagined" (in her case, the "world as meditation") is the "ultimate good." The poem might as appropriately have been titled "Final Soliloquy of the Interior Paramour," since what Penelope comes to see is that she is not only the paramour of the Ulysses of her meditation, but the interior paramour "In an inhuman meditation, larger than her own."

The corresponding passage in "Looking across the Fields and Watching the Birds Fly" (*CP* 517) describes this "pensive nature" as "free / From man's ghost, larger and yet a little like." "Looking across the Fields," which was published in a group with "The World as Meditation," is something of an oddity for *The Rock* in that it reverts to the lightly mocking tone of Stevens' earlier poetry, distancing its speaker from the poet in a way that the surrounding poems do not. Stevens requires this distance because the poem says boldly and unmistakably what "Final Soliloquy" and "The World as Meditation" are able to say only in an equivocal language. Stevens' defense here is not equivocation—although the poem has its difficulties—but the adoption of the faintly pedantic voice of, say, "The Ultimate Poem Is Abstract" or "Study of Images II" of the previous volume, a voice in which Stevens typically exhibits his more whimsical thoughts. A second defense is to attribute the concept of a "pensive nature" to someone else, a Mr. Homburg of Concord, whose name and residence appear to render him a cross between a Schopenhauer-like German philosopher[19] and Ralph Waldo Emerson, although the name also conjures up the image of a rather stuffy gentleman in an old-fashioned hat and suggests the possibility that we are being taken in by humbug. The *humbug* association is perhaps inadvertently more resonant than it may first appear, since a humbug is a thing (or person) that is not really what it pretends to be—an imposture or deception—and "Looking across the Fields" is grounded in a small but crucial pretense.

The deception is that Mr. Homburg and his theory are initially made to appear antithetical to the speaker's (and Stevens') convictions about the nature of reality when in fact he serves as Stevens' spokesman. A number of readers have been taken in by this deception, which is understandable given the manner in which Mr. Homburg is introduced:

> Among the more irritating minor ideas
> Of Mr. Homburg during his visits home
> To Concord, at the edge of things, was this:
>
> To think away the grass, the trees, the clouds,
> Not to transform them into other things,
> Is only what the sun does every day,
>
> Until we say to ourselves that there may be
> A pensive nature, a mechanical
> And slightly detestable *operandum,* free
>
> From man's ghost, larger and yet a little like,
> Without his literature and without his gods . . .

It is easy to see why commentators almost universally identify Mr. Homburg with Emerson—perhaps, Joseph Carroll suggests, the Emerson of "Nature" who "declares that 'man is conscious of a universal soul within or behind his individual life'"—and there is no question that Stevens means to situate his conception in a general tradition of German and American transcendental thought, thus endowing it with a small measure of respectability. But it is charac-terized as a minor idea, not central to transcendental doctrine, and "irritating" to those "at the edge of things"—presumably those provincial minds who have heard it from the great man when he visits his home in Concord. The first stanza does not say, as Carroll believes, that Stevens' "Emersonian persona [is] 'at the edge of things,'" only that Concord is, and it is noteworthy that it is during his visits home, "at the edge of things," that Homburg-Emerson propounds his fanciful notion, as if he, like Stevens, were leery of making it a part of his official canon. Perhaps this is the reason, as Harold Bloom has pointed out, that "the notions attributed to Mr. Homburg do not resemble Emerson's at all."[20]

Carroll believes that Mr. Homburg is depicted as suffering a kind of "spiritual negativity," and it is surprising how many readers of the poem have seen it as Stevens' rejection of the ideas it contem-plates. Gyorgyi Voros characterizes the world that Mr. Homburg posits as "diminished" and "repulsive," and David Michael Hertz argues that the poem depicts a "dehumanization of the connection between matter and mind." Anthony Whiting calls it one of Stevens' "darkest poems," principally because he reads it as a poem about the creative power of the self and concludes that "there is no place in Mr. Homburg's meditation for individual creative activity." Whiting, like many other readers, appears to be working under the assumption that the late poems maintain the exaltation of the indi-vidual imagination Stevens had earlier espoused. This assump-tion—that the epistemology of these last poems is continuous with what preceded them—is also responsible for James Baird's early misreading: "Mr. Homburg of Concord was wrong; spirit does not come from the body of the world (nature); the body of the world comes from the spirit. . . . There are no ideas until the human mind forms them."[21] This indeed would have been Stevens' position a few years earlier, but it is not the position maintained in the poems of *The Rock* and in "Looking across the Fields and Watching the Birds

Fly." Although the opening stanzas are misleading in establishing the poem's attitude toward him, Mr. Homburg was not wrong, and this becomes more apparent as his "fantasia" takes shape.

By the end of the fourth stanza the speaker's sarcasm has disappeared, and he now finds confirmation for Mr. Homburg's "pensive nature." The tone of the poem also shifts from a kind of comic irony to gravity. Some explications of the poem have taken this shift in tone to indicate that Stevens is responding to Mr. Homburg, offering an antithetical conception of nature. Voros believes that "after Stevens disparages Mr. Homburg for making of Nature a senseless operandum, he goes on to depict thought as an instinctual, spontaneous, active force."[22] But the idea that the poem is a debate between Emerson-Homburg and Stevens is difficult to sustain in light of the fact that the later stanzas simply extend the premise attributed to Mr. Homburg at the beginning—that nature is a kind of mind or process of thought. Moreover, in the penultimate stanza the speaker, having dropped the pretense of Mr. Homburg for the nine intervening stanzas, returns to him in his summing up: "Or so Mr. Homburg thought." The gap is similar to that of the early "Sunday Morning," where for forty-odd lines the speaker, deeply absorbed in his argument, appears to forget the woman in the peignoir, the ostensible occasion for the argument, only to return to her abruptly in the final stanza.

Milton Bates is more faithful to the structure of the poem when he notes that it sets out to satirize Mr. Homburg's philosophy "but ends by demonstrating its poetic effectiveness." As the poem proceeds, it "warms to Mr. Homburg's integration and invests it with a highly seductive rhetoric of its own." This is, I believe, the way to read the relationship between Mr. Homburg and the Stevens persona, who takes on the former's philosophy not to refute it but to extend it. It is even possible to mark the moment in the poem when the transfer from Mr. Homburg to Stevens takes place—at line twelve, following the ellipsis, as Hertz has also noted. Bates assumes that Stevens turns against Mr. Homburg at the end since the latter's concept leaves "little scope for spontaneous thought or creativity,"[23] but there is nothing in the poem's conclusion to suggest such a turn. Bates thus joins the long line of readers who cannot accept a Stevens persona who endorses an epistemology in which the poetic imagination is subservient to an external entity "larger and yet a little like."

The poem's shift from mockery to seriousness is similar to that of a well-known contemporary poem, Philip Larkin's "Church Going," in which the Larkin speaker comes to scoff and stays to pray. It is a familiar pattern in Stevens, from the earliest poems such as "Peter Quince at the Clavier" and "Le Monocle de Mon Oncle" onward—the playful title or opening that leads to something unexpectedly earnest. Among Helen Vendler's recommendations for the reader of Stevens are these: "never trust beginnings" and "mistrust titles," the first of which readers of "Looking across the Fields" might well have heeded. Most of its misreadings are the result of placing too much importance on the droll depiction of Mr. Homburg in the first three stanzas and minimizing the significance of the following twelve stanzas, which make up the heart of the poem. After warning readers not to trust Stevens' beginnings, Vendler notes that "the emotional heart of a lyric by Stevens is likely to be found in the middle of the poem,"[24] and so it is with "Looking across the Fields." Its opening portrait of Mr. Homburg is only a strategy for allowing Stevens to pursue with impunity his own fantasia (as he quite correctly terms it), exactly as in "The World as Meditation," where he deflects from himself his seemingly implausible fiction by attributing it to Penelope.

The deflection and the apparent (but not real) irritability in regard to Mr. Homburg are more crucial to "Looking across the Fields," since here Stevens spells out his fantasia at some length and in a specificity not found in the two companion poems. "No doubt we live beyond ourselves in air," the Stevens persona begins after the ellipsis that marks the space between the exposition of Mr. Homburg's concept and Stevens' commentary on it. He has just described Mr. Homburg's "pensive nature" as having an existence separate from the human self, not a product of it but perhaps resembling it, although without our literature, mythologies, or gods. Since nature is not a projection of our selves or our beliefs, it is alien and, at first thought, "slightly detestable"; yet, the speaker reflects, it is obviously true ("No doubt") that we live "beyond ourselves," that we live in a physical world that is not a construct of the human self. It is "beyond" both in being external to the self and in being outside or beyond the genius of the self, the reversal of the epistemology of "The Idea of Order at Key West," where the woman sang "beyond the genius of the sea." One confirmation of the external world's separate and independent existence—and a claim repeated elsewhere in *The Rock*—is that it gives no appearance of being planned or adaptable for our own use. It is

> an element that does not do for us,
> So well, that which we do for ourselves, too big,
> A thing not planned for imagery or belief,
>
> Not one of the masculine myths we used to make. . . .

It does not resemble the supernatural worlds that were a creation of the self because it does not exist to satisfy our human desires. It is beyond or alien to the self in another sense as well; it lacks the sense of form the creative self demands: "A transparency through which the swallow weaves, / Without any form or any sense of form."

Although, as I have indicated, a number of readers have taken the poem's emphasis on the alien quality of Mr. Homburg's pensive nature as a condemnation, it is this very quality—its severance from the human spirit, its existence as cause and not effect—that results in the poem's most ecstatic moment. "The afternoon is visibly a source," the speaker says in affirmation of its separate existence, "Too wide, too irised, to be more than calm, / Too much like thinking to be less than thought." Here again is the world as meditation, although more boldly so than in Penelope's reverie, since "Looking across the Fields" does not depend on "one of the masculine myths we use to make." In "The World as Meditation" Stevens had the returning Ulysses and the meditating Penelope for analogies. Here he relies on a more familiar figure: "Obscurest parent, obscurest patriarch, / A daily majesty of meditation, / That comes and goes in silences of its own." Nature is not only a meditation but a parent or a patriarch, and here again is the apparent paradox that runs through *The Rock.* Struggling to give the external world an existence of its own, he makes it human.

Or so it seems. The analogy is not quite the contradiction that it first appears, since the conclusion of the poem reverses the terms of the parallel between the human and the other. It is not, finally, an instance of depicting the world in human terms, of personifying it. The poem says something much more challenging. It is not that the human mind—thinking, meditating—is a figure for the process of nature; it is rather that the natural process is the source for the workings of the human mind:

> We think, then, as the sun shines or does not.
> We think as wind skitters on a pond in a field
>
> Or we put mantles on our words because
> The same wind, rising and rising, makes a sound
> Like the last muting of winter as it ends.

Earlier the poem had suggested obscurely that Mr. Homburg's pensive nature is the source of "What we know in what we see, what we feel in what / We hear," and finally "what we think." In the later passage it is stated less ambiguously. It is not that the sun (to which is attributed the ability to "think away the grass, the trees, the clouds") is modeled on human thinking, but that, as a cause and not an effect, it provides a model for the process of human thought. It is "visibly a source," and, as in "Not Ideas about the Thing but the Thing Itself," it is privileged over the human. What Robert Pogue Harrison has written of "Not Ideas about the Thing" may be applied to Mr. Homburg's fantasia: it "places us at the heart of the inconceivable priority of nature."[25]

In *The World as Will and Idea*, Schopenhauer had argued that the human will "is of all things the one that is known to us exactly" and that is "exclusively fitted for the explanation of the rest." He thus constructed a model of the external world based on its affinity with the will, declaring that it is "clearly more correct to learn to understand the world from man than man from the world" (*World* 3:471–72). In "Looking across the Fields" Stevens reverses this dictum, attempting to understand man from the world. In a much contested passage his speaker reflects on Mr. Homburg's ideas: "A new scholar replacing an older one reflects / A moment on this fantasia. He seeks / For a human that can be accounted for." Schopenhauer had sought for a world that could be accounted for on the basis of the human; Stevens in "Looking across the Fields" seeks for a human that can be accounted for on the basis of the external world.

This is not to suggest, however, that Stevens is the "new scholar" of this passage, replacing the older Schopenhauer or Emerson. Since Mr. Homburg has so frequently been identified with Emerson, it has been tempting for commentators to equate him with the older scholar now being supplanted by Stevens. He "christens himself 'A new scholar,'" David La Guardia writes, rejecting the "intellective pomposity" of the Mr. Homburg-Emerson figure. Joseph Riddel, Harold Bloom, Milton Bates, and David Michael Hertz all more or less agree, although most of them are not so hard on Emerson. Joseph Carroll agrees up to a point; he believes that what Stevens as the new scholar is attempting to replace is "his older, Emersonian self."[26] The problem with these readings, as pertinent as they might be to a modern poet's assertion of his liberation from a precursor, is that the poem does not support them. In no sense does the poem's position replace Mr. Homburg's; after its playful opening it cites Homburg's fantasia approvingly and offers testimony for its plausibility. Moreover, the context in which Mr. Homburg is alluded to at the poem's conclusion indicates that he is not the older scholar being replaced. Immediately after declaring that the new scholar "seeks / For a human that can be accounted for," Stevens attributes to Mr. Homburg the concept by which the poem has indeed attempted to account for the human: "The spirit comes from the body of the world, / Or so Mr. Homburg thought." It is Mr. Homburg's thought, granting priority to the body of the world over the individual spirit or self, that is the basis of the poem's own reflections. It thus takes a wilful misreading to conclude that Mr. Homburg's thought has been replaced.

Who, then, are the new scholar and the older one? Readers have confused a rhetorical figure with historical personages. What Stevens is suggesting in the trope is the necessity of breaking out of an older paradigm in order to perceive the significance of Mr. Homburg's fantasia—a new self replacing an older one. Ronald Sukenick, who has read the poem more carefully than anyone else to date, puts it well: "A fresh mind willing to consider possibilities in far-fetched ideas . . . considers this speculation, 'this fantasia,' seriously. In it he looks for a description of the human spirit 'that can be accounted for' . . . and in Mr. Homburg's speculation he finds that the spirit can be accounted for as a manifestation of the natural world, as a part of it, and as a response to it."[27] The poem goes a bit further than that in its speculations—to a degree, Sukenick tames it—but he catches its tone and recognizes, as almost no one else does, that Stevens takes Mr. Homburg seriously.

Just how seriously is indicated by the poem's final two stanzas, which incorporate Mr. Homburg:

> The spirit comes from the body of the world,
> Or so Mr. Homburg thought: the body of a world
> Whose blunt laws make an affectation of mind,
>
> The mannerism of nature caught in a glass
> And there become a spirit's mannerism,
> A glass aswarm with things going as far as they can.

In contemporary usage "affectation" carries pejorative connotations, and some readers have seized on the word to argue the shortcomings of the poem's philosophy. "Mr. Homburg concludes his speculation by reversing his opening hypothesis," Anthony Whiting states. "Reality is not 'pensive' but is merely making an 'affectation' of mind." David Michael Hertz agrees, noting the "dehumanization" of the connection between mind and matter, but he assumes that it is nature that displays affectation, that it is nature that is "caught in a glass," that nature has become no more than a "mannerism."[28] Both readings attribute the affectation to the wrong party in the analogy. In the parallel between nature and the human mind, the poem says that the "blunt" laws of nature—explicit, plain, forthright—make the similar working of the human mind seem no more than an affectation; the word is quite precise, since it indicates an artificial or non-natural assumption of behavior. The human mind is to the natural world what a reflection in a mirror is to the real object. The human mind mirrors in a limited way ("things going as far as they can") the larger and prior mannerisms of nature, the poem concludes. It is thus not that nature is being personified or humanized; mannerisms that we think of as human—meditating, thinking, imagining—are not being projected onto nature. The projection moves in the opposite direction, so that our meditating, thinking, imagining owe their pattern to external nature. In "A Collect of Philosophy," delivered the year prior to the publication of the poem, Stevens considers concepts of philosophy that are inherently poetic, and here he has conceived one, a variation on Schopenhauer's world as will discussed in the lecture. And if this new conception is a viable way of conjecturing about our link to the world, as Stevens, through his persona, appears to grant in "Looking across the Fields and Watching the Birds Fly," then it is not surprising that he should compose a poem entitled "The World as Meditation," envision a vast "inhuman meditation," or speculate in "Final Soliloquy of the Interior Paramour" that "The world imagined is the ultimate good." These three poems, along with the title poem and "To an Old Philosopher in Rome," to which I now want to turn, comprise the thematic core of *The Rock*. They bring to the surface, even if in disguise or cloaked in sarcasm, what remains submerged in many of the other late poems.

4 / At the Convent of the Blue Nuns:
"To an Old Philosopher in Rome"

There at the monastery hospital,
you wished those geese-girl sisters wouldn't bother
their heads and yours by praying for your soul:
"There is no God and Mary is His Mother."
—ROBERT LOWELL, "For George Santayana"

IT WAS APPARENTLY IN the late forties that Stevens read Edmund Wilson's *New Yorker* account of a visit to the aged George Santayana in Rome. The article, "Santayana at the Convent of the Blue Nuns," appeared in 1946, and two years later Stevens' paper "Imagination as Value" offered details of Santayana's life at the convent that may reflect Wilson's portrait. More importantly, the *New Yorker* article was incorporated into the most widely admired poem of *The Rock*, "To an Old Philosopher in Rome" (*CP* 508).[1] In recent commentary on the poem, Janet McCann, Thomas Lombardi, and Lea Baechler all assume that Wilson's essay contributed significant details to it, and Baechler examines the intersection between the essay and the poem at some length. She argues that the essay provided "the occasion and the context" for the poem and "provoked Stevens' thinking in a variety of ways." In particular, Wilson's account, like the poem, "particularizes the outer circumstances of Santayana's life and evokes a sense of the quality of his inner spiritual life."[2]

It is relatively easy to detect, as Baechler does, links between the two texts. Both writers contrast the busy life of the city and its architecture—Stevens' "bird-nest arches" and "rain-stained-vaults"—to the simplicity and bareness of Santayana's room inside the convent. Wilson writes, "He occupied a single room, in which he both worked and slept. There was a table at his right, with papers and books, and, at his left, a small bed, concealed by a screen. There was almost nothing else in the room." In the poem the simple objects of Santayana's room and the ever-present nuns—"The bed, the books, the chair, the moving nuns"—are transformed into a trope of the austerity of Santayana's life at the end—what Stevens here and elsewhere names "poverty"—to which the poem keeps returning, as in the penultimate stanza:

> It is a kind of total grandeur at the end,
> With every visible thing enlarged and yet
> No more than a bed, a chair and moving nuns. . . .

The realistic details of Santayana's immediate surroundings are used to indicate a larger, more imaginative vision. As Baechler points out, Wilson also anticipates this merging of the real and the imaginative. "The image of him came back to me afterward," Wilson writes,

> in the course of the solitary evenings that I spent when I was first in Rome, alone, with his plain table and his narrow bed, so far from Spain and from Harvard, yet with all the philosophies, the religions, and the poetry through which he had passed making about him an iridescent integument, the manners of all the societies in which he had sojourned awhile supplying him with pictures and phrases; a shell of faded skin and frail bone, in which the power of intellect, the colors of imagination stilled burned.

The passage indicates another connection with the poem not detectable in any one image or detail but in the tone of the essay as a whole—the reverence with which Santayana's "dignity and his distinction" are depicted, the "readiness and grace with which he lived up to a classical role."[3]

Baechler's extensive examination of the bond between the two texts is entirely convincing, and yet there is a curious omission in her discussion. She passes over the essay's conclusion and its arresting final image, which appears to lie behind the poem's major theme, its depiction of Santayana as living simultaneously in two worlds. Near the end of the essay Wilson notes that even in the isolation of the convent Santayana is not "really alone in the sense that the ordinary person would be." He remains in "the world of men" through his reading and writing, since "the intelligence that has persisted in him has been the intelligence of the civilized human race." The essay concludes, "He has made it his business to extend himself into every kind of human consciousness with which he could establish contact, and he reposes in his shabby chaise longue like a monad in the universal mind."[4]

The image of Santayana in his shabby chair in a bare convent room in Rome existing at the same time as a particle in a larger world figured as a universal mind clearly lies behind "To an Old Philosopher in Rome," just as the concept of living at once in two worlds is central to the poems of *The Rock* as a whole. This is clear from the first line of *The Rock*'s opening poem, "An Old Man Asleep" (*CP* 501)—"The two worlds are asleep, are sleeping now." The poem, apparently written in the same year as "To an Old Philosopher in Rome," 1952,[5] may itself have absorbed Wilson's portrait of Santayana. (Santayana, like the old man of the opening poem, is "dozing in the depths of wakefulness," "alive / Yet living in two worlds.") The two worlds are also present in the other poems published in the *Hudson Review* in 1952 with "To an Old Philosopher in Rome," most strikingly "Looking across the Fields and Watching the Birds Fly" and "The World as Meditation." When read together, these poems imply that one of Stevens' principal explorations involves a perception of reality as the contents of a universal mind. In "The World as Meditation" this insight is conferred on Penelope; in "Looking across the Fields and Watching the Birds Fly" it is credited to the Emerson-like Mr. Homburg of Concord. Here it is the aged Santayana, on the threshold of death, who is allowed to experience what the aged narrator of other poems of *The Rock* hints at but treats most explicitly when attributed to someone else. "To an Old Philosopher in Rome" is thus central to the project of the late poems, since it depicts a Stevens surrogate who has, as its last line makes clear, *realized* an imaginative projection to the extent that he is able to live within it and find solace in the destitution of old age.

That Santayana speaks in some sense for the poet-narrator and that the Stevens of *The Rock*—on the threshold of death, as he has constructed himself—sees himself in Santayana are hardly in question. "Santayana becomes a surrogate for Stevens himself," Harold Bloom writes, while Baechler argues that "in contemplating the 'dying' and imminent death of another, Stevens confronts his own." Charles Berger, dissenting from this view in a lengthy discussion of the poem, argues that Stevens does not identify with Santayana, who dies as the philosopher, not the poet. Stevens' praise is, finally, "eulogistic of another, rather than prescriptive for himself."[6] Yet Berger's perception is clearly contradicted by the poem's narrator, who frankly addresses Santayana as a surrogate, not only for himself but for all those on the threshold. He asks the dying philosopher to speak "with an accurate tongue" of the "pity" that is "the memorial" of his convent room, "so that each of us / Beholds himself in you, and hears his voice / In yours." It is an ironic self-reference to Stevens' appropriation of Santayana in the poem, since of course Santayana can do nothing other than speak for the poet who has provided him both his words and his vision.

A further irony outside the poem testifies to the degree to which the circumstances of Santayana's death were in fact prescriptive for Stevens. Thomas Lombardi observes that "To an Old Philosopher in Rome" prefigures Stevens' own death: "Santayana, without religious faith through most of his life, had lived out his last days with the Blue Nuns in a Roman convent, as Stevens himself at the end would be tended by nuns in Saint Francis Hospital." Both unbelievers "died in a place of faith," although Stevens' controversial conversion seems to indicate that they responded to these spiritual places quite differently. Wilson records Santayana as remarking that "someone had said about him . . . that he himself was a Catholic in everything but faith,"[7] and Robert Lowell catches this paradox in his poem "For George Santayana"—"'There is no God and Mary is His Mother.'" Although he uses the language of religion, Stevens appears less interested in the purely religious implications of Santayana's liminal experience in the convent than in its larger theoretical significance, its confirmation of the fiction that pervades the last poems, the world as meditation.

It is not as a religious figure that Santayana is conceived in the poem, but as a thinker and writer among his books, an aesthetician (although Santayana was uneasy about the term)[8] whose own life has been fashioned almost as a work of art. This is Wilson's conception of Santayana, which Stevens also advances in his discussion of Santayana in "Imagination as Value," a paper written not long after the *New Yorker* article appeared. In the paper Stevens attempts to demonstrate the value of the imagination in life as opposed to its value in arts and letters. While most men's lives "are thrust upon them," there are nonetheless lives "which exist by the deliberate choice of those that live them":

> To use a single illustration: it may be assumed that the life of Professor Santayana is a life in which the function of the imagination has had a function similar to its function in any deliberate work of art or letters. We have only to think of this present phase of it, in which, in his old age, he dwells in the head of the world, in the company of devoted women, in their convent, and in the company of familiar saints, whose presence does so much to make any convent appropriate refuge for a generous and human philosopher. To repeat, there can be lives in which the value of the imagination is the same as its value in arts and letters. (*NA* 147–48)

The passage serves as another significant intertext for "To an Old Philosopher in Rome," and what it brings to the surface is the degree to which the vision granted to Santayana in the poem is fundamentally aesthetic or imaginative. Although it is cloaked in the religious language that its setting demands, what engages the narrator is the manner in which the contents of an imaginative mind are made real—"As if the design of all his words takes form / And frame from thinking and is realized."

Stevens' idealization of Santayana as the saint of thinkers may also owe something to their personal relationship. Stevens knew him as a kind of unofficial adviser at Harvard, "when I was a boy and when he was not yet in mid-life" (*Letters* 482). Santayana invited the young student to come to see him a number of times, Stevens read poems to him, and the two famously exchanged sonnets about cathedrals built along the sea. In the year before Wilson's article on Santayana appeared, Stevens remembered that at Harvard Santayana's "mind was full of the great projects of his future and, while some of these have been realized, it is possible to think that many have not." (In the poem Santayana's thoughts are realized in a quite different way.) In the same letter Stevens attempts to define what part Santayana played in his apprenticeship as a poet, implying that he filled the role of mentor and master poet, perhaps something like the relationship between poet and ephebe depicted in "Notes toward a Supreme Fiction": "I always came away from my visits to him feeling that he made up in the most genuine way for many things that I needed. He was then still definitely a poet" (*Letters* 482).[9] Santayana was not a poet in the convent of the Blue Nuns, and Stevens' title reminds us that it is not a poem about the death of a poet. But then it is not exactly a poem about a dying philosopher. "Santayana is not a philosopher in any austere sense," Stevens wrote in 1949 (*Letters* 647). Santayana's importance for Stevens both in the poem and in "Imagination as Value" is not simply that he produced philosophical theories, that he was a thinker, but that his thought shaped his own life, to such an extent that his life became analogous to a work of the imagination, like a text made real. That is why he is elected to receive the vision to which Stevens keeps returning in the surrounding poems of *The Rock*.

What exactly is the nature of the vision Santayana receives "On the threshold of heaven"? Stevens' elusive depiction of it leaves some room for disagreement. Alan Perlis believes that at the point of death Santayana has achieved a perspective in which "the objects of this world shrink to insignificance" and all things "are a part of his self." Kathleen Woodward argues the opposite, that Santayana transcends himself, losing the sense of self in becoming a figure of heaven. Lucy Beckett writes that "Stevens is here very near to a spiritual centre, a point of rest, that could as well be described in the traditional terms of Christian theology," while Margaret Peterson sees the poem as "a tribute by an atheist poet to an atheist philosopher." A "Christian reading," she argues, "would destroy the point of the poem—which depends upon a rather exact knowledge of Santayana's contribution to the problem of knowledge." Lea Baechler describes the process Santayana undergoes as an act of "transubstantiation," the "transubstantiating power" constituting "an act of imagination." Yet Charles Berger finds that the "central personage in 'To an Old Philosopher in Rome' treats his approaching death reasonably"—that is, as the philosopher—and that his "discovery of the realm of 'another' lacks the true *otherness* displayed in 'The Owl in the Sarcophagus.'"[10] If the "Old Philosopher" shares the vision described in other poems of *The Rock,* however, it comes to him not only because he is a philosopher but because he is old. "It is poverty's speech that seeks us out the most," and the poverty here, as elsewhere in *The Rock,* is the poverty of old age. Santayana, that is, shares a great deal with other personae of *The Rock,* both in the nature of his insight and the circumstance under which it is attained.

To state it most simply (and in a manner which will need to be amplified later), Santayana's insight is the experience of living in two worlds, and the circumstance under which it is attained is the poverty of life at the end. One of the misconceptions about "To an Old Philosopher in Rome" is that what Santayana experiences is a vision of the afterlife. Margaret Peterson notes that the "first stanza seemingly introduces a vision by a dying philosopher about to enter a Christian heaven." Although she is aware that our first impression is deceptive, other readers have also treated the poem as Santayana's imaginative encounter with a kind of heaven to come. Charles

Berger's influential reading speaks of the poem's speculations "about the spirit's final resting place," its "refusal to push too far into an afterlife," and "the order Santayana prepares to join." Gyorgyi Voros reads the poem as "a moment of suspension between the completion of one form of dwelling and the start of another," and she writes that Santayana "experiences a constant superimposition of the physical world he knows on to the approaching afterworld, which, uncannily, it seems he knows almost as well."[11] The setting in a convent in Rome and Stevens' use of terms such as *heaven, spirit,* and *celestial* all contribute to this view, but other parts of the poem contradict it, and it would be inconsistent for Stevens to attribute to the nonbeliever Santayana a desire for a conventional Christian heaven. What the poem does is to allow its setting and its subject's lifelong obsession with Catholicism to dictate the terms of its depiction of his experience, which is something much more radical than a traditional view of a Christian afterlife.

The experience that Stevens attributes to the dying philosopher is clarified to a degree if we read the poem against certain of Santayana's own texts, not as sources—one important text was published after the poem—but as intertexts that help to focus our reading. Among the most helpful of these are Santayana's three-volume memoir *Persons and Places,* which Stevens owned, and *Interpretations of Poetry and Religion,* which was published during Stevens' last year at Harvard. In a *New Yorker* review of the first volume of *Persons and Places* (published two years before his interview with Santayana in Rome), Edmund Wilson calls it "the most remarkable book of its kind since Yeats's 'Autobiographies.'" He points out that few first-rate writers have produced memoirs that are among their major works; only Yeats and Henry Adams, he believes, have created something comparable. The value of the first volume of *Persons and Places* is that it "gives us something that the author had not got out in his other works: not merely the facts of his career but a searching and subtle study of the meaning for him of his experience."[12] This is also the value of the memoir for the reader of "To an Old Philosopher in Rome," since the poem attempts, through an

act of imagination, to assess the meaning for Santayana of his expe-
rience of old age while remaining faithful to Santayana's own mode
of thought.

One perhaps superficial and fortuitous indication of Stevens'
faithfulness to Santayana's manner of conceiving his experience
may be seen in the verbal parallels between the two texts. For
Stevens, the essential element of Santayana's vision is liminality,
and the poem begins and ends on the threshold:

> On the threshold of heaven, the figures in the street
> Become the figures of heaven, the majestic movement
> Of men growing small in the distances of space,
> Singing, with smaller and still smaller sound,
> Unintelligible absolution and an end—
>
> The threshold, Rome, and that more merciful Rome
> Beyond, the two alike in the make of the mind.
> It is as if in a human dignity
> Two parallels become one, a perspective, of which
> Men are part both in the inch and in the mile.

In the third volume of *Persons and Places* Santayana begins his
chapter "Old Age in Italy" with the same trope: "When at the
threshold of old age I found myself free and looked about for a
place of retirement and finally found it in Italy and particularly in
Rome, I was not at all in search of an ideal society or even of a con-
genial one." What he was searching for, he writes, was a place
"where I might bring my life to a peaceful end" (*Persons* 3:119).
Stevens' poem speaks of "The threshold, Rome, and that more mer-
ciful Rome / Beyond," and Santayana is himself aware of having
created a more "merciful" Rome. Describing his visual impressions
of the sights of Rome, he notes that many of them "depended on
the time of day and the weather for their full effect"; but the effect
of a Rome beyond the actual came from himself, he writes, with his
"imperfect eyesight wrapping everything in a second often merci-

ful atmosphere" (*Persons* 3:129). There is no question of actual influence in this instance, since the third volume of *Persons and Places* did not appear until after Santayana's death, long after "To an Old Philosopher in Rome" had been published.[13]

There is yet another striking evocation of Santayana's thought in the second stanza of "To an Old Philosopher in Rome." Here, as elsewhere in the poem, Stevens wishes to indicate that what Santayana glimpses on the threshold is not a totally separate world or a future world but a simultaneous parallel world, in which the objects of his immediate surroundings are seen in a different light. The clearest instance of such simultaneity occurs in the penultimate stanza, where the "total grandeur at the end" entails "every visible thing enlarged and yet / No more than a bed, a chair and moving nuns." The two Romes of the second stanza are said to be "alike in the make of the mind." It is as if "Two parallels become one, a perspective, of which / Men are part both in the inch and in the mile." In Santayana's terminology, one might say that the men are seen both in their existence and in their essence. Existence and essence form a key binary in Santayana's philosophy. Existence is contingent, arbitrary, accidental; essence is the realm of the mind, the imagination, or what he frequently calls the spirit. As Richard C. Lyon puts it: "It is the nature of the mind to outrun in its conceiving what merely happens to exist or to have once existed. Its native vocation lies in ranging beyond the facts, beyond even the facts of the history of the human imagination, into the infinite region of possibles which Santayana called the realm of essence."[14]

In *Apologia Pro Mente Sua* Santayana recalls that his Harvard teacher Josiah Royce once told him that the gist of his philosophy was the separation of essence from existence (*Philosophy* 497). His response, some pages later, is that he does not separate them but merely distinguishes between them. They cannot be separated, he argues, because they are not continuous. His example adopts the same figure as the second stanza of the poem:

But nothing can ever make existence and essence continuous, as nothing can ever make architecture continuous with music: like parallels such orders of being can never flow into one another.

But they may be conjoined or superposed; they may be simultaneous dimensions of the same world. (*Philosophy* 525)

Margaret Peterson, who cites this passage in Santayana, argues that Stevens renders the philosophical distinction precisely, and she notes as well that by labeling the perception as a peculiarly "human perspective," Stevens is echoing Santayana's theory that to perceive essences "was a uniquely human act as opposed to an animal function, an act by which man transcended his animal existence for the moral life of 'spirit.'"[15] What manner of transcendence is suggested in the poem is not apparent at this point, but what is clear is the simultaneity of the two Romes, which are simply seen on different scales, "in the inch and in the mile."

But what are we to make of these different scales, of Stevens' spatial metaphor in the opening of the poem, "the majestic movement / Of men growing small in the distances of space," men who "are part both in the inch and in the mile"? Later the poem sees the "veritable small" in the "illumined large" and concludes with the "Total grandeur of a total edifice." Richard C. Lyon reverses my perspective in his introduction to the critical edition of *Persons and Places,* using "To an Old Philosopher in Rome" as a way of reading Santayana's memoir. He notes Stevens' spatial metaphor and observes, "In *Persons and Places* Santayana himself employs a spatial, a geographic metaphor to explain his life and mind," although, as he also notes, this metaphor does not emerge explicitly until the third volume. Yet Stevens' spatial metaphor has to do not so much with geography as with size. One of Santayana's worlds is large, the other small, although this distinction itself has generated some confusion. The conventional reading is that objects are small in the existing world, large in Santayana's imaginative world. Alan Perlis writes, as I have noted, that from Santayana's vantage point on the threshold of heaven, "the objects of this world shrink to insignificance," while Margaret Peterson reads the men who are part "both in the inch and in the mile" as suggesting that in "the realm of possible essences," the men "may be idealized into a more grandiose vision."[16] The poem plays with the notion of perspective throughout, but in its opening stanzas it is the inch and not the mile that is associated with Santayana's idealized vision, and recognizing this perspective is pivotal in understanding the nature of the vision.

When, in the first stanza, the figures in the street become the figures of heaven, the pattern is one of diminishment and distancing—"the majestic movement / Of men growing small in the distances of space." Their sounds too become "smaller and still smaller," until they are finally unintelligible. The "muttering" of the newsboys of the fourth stanza becomes the more distant "murmuring"; the sharp, immediate smell of medicine, distanced, becomes "a fragrantness not to be spoiled." In such a vision the actual men in the mile become, in the larger expanse, men in the inch. Because of the vastness of the world that Santayana imagines—a totality, a vision of the whole—the men who inhabit it are, in the new perspective, infinitesimally small. The metaphor of largeness is thus used in seemingly contradictory ways in the poem. In one sense, "every visible thing [is] enlarged," achieving its place in a "total grandeur at the end," yet from the perspective of this total grandeur, its place in the whole becomes smaller. When the speaker says in the eighth stanza, "we feel, in this illumined large, / The veritable small, so that each of us / Beholds himself in you," the large is the total vision and the small is the speaker's, or Santayana's place in it.

It is as if, at the end, Santayana has been able, like the cosmic imagination that inhabits so many of Stevens' late poems, to realize, to make real, a purely imaginative world, the contents of a mind. This bold possibility, hinted at throughout the poem, is made clear only in the final two stanzas:

> It is a kind of total grandeur at the end,
> With every visible thing enlarged and yet
> No more than a bed, a chair and moving nuns,
> The immensest theatre, the pillared porch,
> The book and candle in your ambered room,
>
> Total grandeur of a total edifice,
> Chosen by an inquisitor of structures

For himself. He stops upon this threshold,
As if the design of all his words takes form
And frame from thinking and is realized.

Edmund Wilson ends his *New Yorker* essay with Santayana reposing "in his shabby chaise longue like a monad in the universal mind," and in the poem Stevens has him achieve a similar vision. This "inquisitor of structures" has finally imagined the "Total grandeur of a total edifice," in which the "design" of his thought "takes form" and "is realized." The conclusion accentuates the totality of Santayana's created edifice. It is a complete world that he has realized, in which the objects of his partial world—"a bed, a chair and moving nuns"—take their place, thereby enlarging their meaning, clarifying their significance, even though they are "No more than a bed, a chair and moving nuns." To see an object as "a monad in the universal mind" does not change the nature of the object but simply alters the perspective from which it is viewed, which helps to explain the extent to which "To an Old Philosopher in Rome" is a poem about perspectives, things seen both in the inch and in the mile, a world seen both as a collection of physical objects and as the contents of an imagination "realized," made real.

Santayana's versions and explications of the experience Stevens ascribes to him in the poem may be found throughout his works, most notably in the late memoir *Persons and Places* but in earlier texts as well. In "A General Confession," for example, he anticipates Stevens' depiction of a vision in which "every visible thing [is] enlarged and yet / No more than a bed, a chair and moving nuns." Defending his concept of essences, Santayana notes that they "exercise no control over the existing world," yet through their agency "the actuality of things is sharpened and the possibilities of things are enlarged" (*Philosophy* 29, 30). In *Apologia Pro Mente Sua* he writes, "An essence is an 'idea,' but an idea lifted out of its immersion in existing objects and in existing feelings; so that when considered in itself and recognised as a pure essence its very clarity seems to strip both objects and feelings of their familiar lights: reality becomes mysterious and appearance becomes unreal." He continues, "My theory ought to be intelligible to poets and artists" (*Philosophy* 500), and indeed it was intelligible to Stevens, who uses it, or something very like it, as the basis for his concepts of the "first idea" and seeing an object "in the idea of it" in the opening cantos of "Notes toward a Supreme Fiction" (*CP* 380).

Stevens addresses Santayana in "To an Old Philosopher in Rome" as "a citizen of heaven though still of Rome," and in *Interpretations of Poetry and Religion* Santayana, in discussing the early Christians, explains this circumstance. As Stevens does elsewhere, he argues that religion is "a poetry in which men believe" (*IPR* 21): "It was a whole world of poetry descended among men, like the angels at the Nativity, doubling, as it were, their habitation, so that they might move through supernatural realms in the spirit while they walked the earth in the flesh" (*IPR* 56). Like poets, the early Christians "sought to stimulate their imaginations, to focus, as it were, the long vistas of an invisible landscape" (*IPR* 56). And the most successful of these, the saints, became permanent "citizens" of the supernatural world they imagined: "In the saint, in the soul that had become already the perpetual citizen of that higher sphere, nothing in this world remained without reference to the other, nor was anything done save for a supernatural end." In such a state, as one feels of Santayana in the poem, "death itself could bring but a slight and unessential change of environment" (*IPR* 57). *Interpretations of Poetry and Religion* is perhaps more than an intertext by which to read "To an Old Philosopher in Rome"; it appears to be a source, in the conventional sense, for some of the philosophical and religious concepts that underlie Stevens' poetry, as Milton Bates and Margaret Peterson have argued.

Interpretations of Poetry and Religion appeared during Stevens' last year at Harvard, and an unsigned review of it was published in the *Harvard Advocate* while Stevens was its editor. Bates says that it is unknown whether Stevens actually read the book; however, there is evidence that he knew of it and discussed it with Santayana. Stevens recorded (on the blank back pages of his copy of Santayana's *Lucifer*) an evening spent with Santayana and Pierre la Rose, who was also connected with the Harvard English Department. Among other things, they read and debated an unfavorable review of *Interpretations of Poetry and Religion* that had appeared in *The Nation*—"Santayana took it good-naturedly"—and discussed the book's chapter on Emerson. This was presumably Stevens' final meeting with Santayana before leaving Harvard. His account concludes, "We smoked cigarettes, drank whisky etc. until eleven when we broke up. I shall probably not see him again."[17]

Stevens told Barbara Church that he "knew [Santayana] well" at Harvard (*Letters* 761), and in his introduction to the critical edition of *Interpretations of Poetry and Religion* Joel Porte calls Stevens "Santayana's truest disciple, his most constant ephebe."[18] Yet in his chapter titled "Younger Harvard Friends" in the second volume of *Persons and Places*, Santayana does not mention Stevens,[19] although the volume contains an explanation of sorts for the omission. "I have commemorated many American friends, and not one man of letters, not one poet," Santayana writes. "The poets and the learned men remained, for the most part, in the category of acquaintances. There may have been a professional feminine jealousy between us that prevented a frank and hearty comradeship" (*Persons* 2:148). In its honesty in such matters and in its ability to allow us glimpses of his thoughts and feelings, *Persons and Places* is the Santayana text most useful to a reader of "To an Old Philosopher in Rome." Written in the convent of the Blue Nuns, it exhibits a sensibility Stevens appropriates and heightens in the poem.

"That the real was rotten and only the imaginary at all interesting seemed to me axiomatic," Santayana writes of his youth in the first volume of *Persons and Places*, adding that "allowing for the rash generalizations of youth, it is still what I think. My philosophy has never changed" (*Persons* 1:172). He was by nature a transcendentalist, he now recognizes: "I think there was a congenital transcendentalism in me, long before I heard of transcendental philosophy or understood it. I had a spontaneous feeling that life is a dream. The scene might entirely disappear at any moment, or be entirely transformed" (*Persons* 1:176). Religion appealed to him more than any other area of life "precisely because religion, like poetry, was more ideal, more freely imaginary, and in a material sense falser"

(*Persons* 1:174). And there are moments, especially in the third volume of *Persons and Places,* when Santayana describes the kind of visions the imagination creates, in which the existing world gives way to an ideal world of essences. He recounts, for example, a characteristic experience in Rome, where "being old and fond of sitting upon public benches," he rests in front of the cathedral of San Giovanni: "In those calm moments my eye has learned to frame wonderful vistas in that great church, forward to the restored apse with its golden mosaics and its papal throne, or across aisles and aisles, into side chapels, each a church in itself." He continues, "And then the whole place seems to lose its rigidity and its dead pomp, and to become a marvellous labyrinth, as if it were a work of nature or of fancy rather than of human art." What is disappointing in the real church, "the moderate height," changes to "a condition of unlimited breadth." The ceiling is transformed to a "soaring dome," and "you see beyond, quite subordinate to this rectangular space, soaring domes and vaults, enclosing other spaces and shedding variously coloured lights on other elaborate altars" (*Persons* 3:129–30).

Santayana argues that the imagination, or the "spirit," as he most often refers to it,[20] is heightened in old age. At the end of the chapter titled "Old Age in Italy" he discusses the gifts of age in a manner that recalls Stevens' "total grandeur at the end." "Nothing is inherently and invincibly young except spirit," he writes. "And spirit can enter a human being perhaps better in the quiet of old age and dwell there more undisturbed than in the turmoil of adventure." The genius of old age, he adds, is that it sees beyond its own private center and attains a vision of the whole:

> In Rome, in the eternal city, I feel nearer to my own past, and to the whole past and future of the world. . . . Old places and old persons in their turn, when spirit dwells in them, have an intrinsic vitality of which youth is incapable; precisely the balance and wisdom that comes from long perspectives and broad foundations. Everything shines then for the spirit by its own light in its own place and time; but not as it shone in its own restless eyes. For in its own eyes each person and each place was the centre of

a universe full of threatening and tempting things; but old age, having less intensity at the centre has more clearness at the cir-cumference, and knows that just because spirit, at each point, is a private centre for all things, no one point, no one phase of spirit is materially a public centre for all the rest. Thus recogni-tion and honour flow out to all things, from the mind that con-ceives them justly and without egotism; and thus mind is recon-ciled to its own momentary existence and limited vision by the sense of the infinite supplements that embosom it on every side. (*Persons* 3:131–32)

Although published after "To an Old Philosopher in Rome," this passage nonetheless informs the poem in suggesting the concept of the spirit the poem depicts. "Things dark on the horizons of per-ception, / Become accompaniments of fortune," Stevens writes, but "of the fortune of the spirit, beyond the eye."

Persons and Places informs Stevens' portrait of Santayana, both inside and outside the poem, in other ways. In "Imagination as Value," Stevens had used Santayana's as an example of a life in which the imagination functions as in a work of art. *Persons and Places* makes a similar claim. In "A Change of Heart," the opening chapter of the third volume (published separately as an essay in 1948), Santayana defines the "purity" of one's art as "the degree to which [one's] art has become his life" (*Persons* 3:2), and a principle that applies to one's philosophy as well; Santayana's claim is "I *lived* my philosophy" (*Persons* 3:10). In the poem Stevens depicts San-tayana as "impenitent" in his attitude toward the church, and in "A Change of Heart" Santayana explains at some length why "a truly free spirit will never repent" (*Persons* 3:2).[21] More importantly "A Change of Heart" establishes a link between passion, wisdom, and despair that is touched on elsewhere in *Persons and Places* and oper-ates as one of the assumptions of "To an Old Philosopher in Rome."

Richard C. Lyon says that *Persons and Places* is "the story of San-tayana's difficult extrication of his spirit from the meshes of cir-cumstance in which he found himself."[22] In "A Change of Heart" Santayana describes his life in "the clinic of the Blue Sisters upon the Caelius." He has distributed his few possessions, renounced "chattels of every kind," abstained from the good food and drink in which he once indulged, and lives contentedly "in solitude and confinement" (*Persons* 3:7). He traces his present circumstances to an earlier personal crisis, or *metanoia* as he terms it, in which his friendships, his ambitions, his career as a professor of philosophy no longer had meaning for him. In releasing his claims on life, however, he discovered another dimension, another world. He had achieved a transition "from the many to the one, from the existent but transitory to the ideal and eternal." Such a transition, like the tragic catharsis, "turns disaster into a kind of rapture without those false comforts and delusions by which religious *metanoia* is often cheapened" (*Persons* 3:8). "There is therefore enthusiasm no less than resignation in an enlightened *metanoia*," he writes. "You give up everything in the form of claims; you receive everything back in the form of a divine presence" (*Persons* 3:12). Although his epiphany initially involved no visible change in his mode of living, henceforth his experience was colored by his "passage through dark night," and he discovered that "the truth of life could be seen only in the shadow of death; living and dying were simultaneous and inseparable" (*Persons* 3:13). He composed a sequence of sonnets on the experience, in which, he says, the "key to the whole is given in the one line: *A perfect love is founded on despair*" (*Persons* 3:14). "A Change of Heart" ends with the soul's acquisition of "a peace which is an orchestration of transcended sorrows" (*Persons* 3:15), and the final chapter of *Persons and Places* speaks of the spirit turning the "sorrows of nature into glimpses of eternal truth" (*Persons* 3:144).

Santayana consequently anticipates one of the themes of "To an Old Philosopher in Rome" and *The Rock* as a whole—the insight, the clarity of vision that may be traced directly to renunciation, misery, and destitution. "The whole world belongs to me implicitly when I have given it all up, and am wedded to nothing particular in it," Santayana writes in "A Change of Heart," "but for the same reason no part of it properly belongs to me as a possession, but all only in idea." Of this insight, he adds, "I came to clearness about it only

in my old age" (*Persons* 3:5). Stevens' portrait of Santayana is built
on his destitution; he is confined to a convent room with a bed, a
table, and a chair. "It is poverty's speech that seeks us out the most,"
he records, and Santayana speaks it "without speech." It is spoken
by the manner in which he chose to end his life, to exchange a world
as a possession for a world as thought. The grandeur that he finds
in a world that "takes form . . . from thinking and is realized" thus
has its origin in the poverty of the material world. This is the idea
that lies behind a difficult passage in the poem in which the Stevens
persona, speaking directly to Santayana, tells him that he can find
the grandeur that he needs only "in misery." Santayana is "alive,"

> Yet living in two worlds, impenitent
> As to one, and, as to one, most penitent,
> Impatient for the grandeur that you need
>
> In so much misery; and yet finding it
> Only in misery, the afflatus of ruin,
> Profound poetry of the poor and of the dead. . . .

Santayana is thus the prototype of other old men in *The Rock*, par-
ticularly the persona of "Final Soliloquy of the Interior Paramour"
(*CP* 524), who in his poverty achieves a similar vision of "an order,
a whole," and the persona of "Lebensweisheitspielerei" (*CP* 504),
who in his indigence glimpses the "stale grandeur of annihilation,"
a phrase that, except for the "stale," might have come from "To an
Old Philosopher in Rome." But his presence is not limited to these
texts. The spirit of Santayana in the convent of the Blue Nuns seems
to haunt Stevens' last poems. "Do any human beings ever realize life
while they live it?" the Stage Manager is asked in Thornton Wilder's
Our Town. "No," he responds, and then, after a pause, "The saints
and poets, maybe—they do some."[23] In *The Rock* Stevens places
Santayana as the secular saint (and himself as the poet) in this illus-
trious company, although he restricts the circumstances in which
realization may take place. Santayana provides him the model for

what it is to devote one's life to words and ideas, as Stevens had devoted himself to conceptions of a supreme fiction, and what it is to have them take form and be realized finally in the poverty and clarity of life's end.

5 / Reconstructing "The Rock":
Stevens and Misreading

Does the necessity of misreading mean the same thing in each case? . . . Even if the law of misreading applies here also, there are obviously strong and weak critical misreadings, more or less vital ones.
—J. HILLIS MILLER, "Deconstructing the Deconstructers"

There are weak mis-readings and strong mis-readings, just as there are weak poems and strong poems, but there are no right readings, because reading a text is necessarily the reading of a whole system of texts, and meaning is always wandering around between texts.
—HAROLD BLOOM, Kabbalah and Criticism

THE TWO LONG POEMS OF *The Rock*—To an Old Philosopher in Rome" and the title poem—have been the least accessible for readers, in part because they have not generally been read in relation to the collection as a whole. "The Rock," in particular, has acquired a distinction quite apart from its place in the collection, and I want to look at that in some detail before attempting to restore it to its place. The poem played a small but significant role in the institutionalization of deconstructive criticism, although its part in the brief history of American deconstruction is complicated by a fundamental confusion or incoherence that may be located in J. Hillis Miller's influential 1976 reading, the text that assigned its role. Miller used the poem as the foundation for one of the earliest attempts to introduce to the uninitiated what was then known primarily as the Yale School, a group of what Miller called "uncanny critics," consisting of himself, Harold Bloom, Paul de Man, Geoffrey Hartman, and Jacques Derrida. As Robert Markley (among others) has noted, Miller's two-part essay, published in the *Georgia Review* as "Stevens' Rock and Criticism as Cure," is now recognized as one of the seminal statements of his version of deconstruction. Recounting the beginnings of American deconstruction in *After the New Criticism*, Frank Lentricchia observes that among Derrida's followers "Miller assumed the burden of chief spokesman and polemicist." And while de Man was producing a series of "Derridean revisions of Nietzsche" and "Hartman was establishing himself as the philological athlete of American poststructuralism," Miller took on one of the spokesmen for traditional criticism, M. H. Abrams, at the Modern Language Association convention and in *Critical Inquiry* and "prepared a long two-part essay on Wallace Stevens for the *Georgia Review* (in the course of which he carried Stevens into the poststructuralist camp)."[1]

The *Georgia Review* essay became one of the principal statements in the early dissemination of deconstructive criticism for a number of reasons, not the least of which is its brilliantly wrong-headed reading of "The Rock." But it was also the clearest and strongest statement to that point on the program of literary deconstruction. It is perhaps the central text in Vincent Leitch's and William E. Cain's early attempts to estimate Miller's criticism, and Abrams refers to it repeatedly in his MLA confrontation with Miller. Cain's 1979 essay finds that it is one of two texts in which Miller "elaborates his deconstructive stance in greatest detail." (The other is his review of Joseph Riddel's *The Inverted Bell*, to which I will return.) Leitch's essay, published a few months later, characterizes Miller's description of the "means and ends" of deconstruction in the second part of the article as "the most lucid account yet written." Lentricchia, focusing on the article's polemical nature, observes that in it Miller "introduced a key term for the controversy, *mise en abyme*, reviewed the state of American and Continental criticism, and inducted his Yale colleagues into the uncanny critics' hall of fame."[2]

Because of its central place among the early texts of deconstructive criticism, I want to reread "Stevens' Rock and Criticism as Cure" together with some of these texts and, most importantly, Stevens' poem. Now that we are in the wake of deconstructive literary criticism (as distinguished from Derridean deconstruction), its moment of putative dominance in the academy having passed,[3] elements of Miller's strategy and style that have been obscured may perhaps be more easily read, in the way that any critical practice or ideology opens itself to remoteness. Although deconstructive readings of Miller's kind are no longer central to critical practice, their influence remains, just as formalist assumptions and strategies survived the demise of formalism. My assumption is that both Stevens' poem, which has been shaped by Miller's preemptive reading,[4] and Miller's theory of misreading, which seeks its sanction in the poem, will be illuminated by a reexamination of the relationship between the poem and the essay and between these texts and other early texts of deconstructive criticism—a reexamination of the meaning, as Harold Bloom says, that "is always wandering around between texts."[5] This will necessitate a somewhat lengthy detour through Miller's early deconstructive theory and practice before arriving at "The Rock." (Readers who are easily bored by excursions into literary theory may advance directly to the discussion of the poem, although deconstruction offers some unusually engaging twists and turns.)

How may a theory of reading be illuminated by attention to its practical application? What is the relation between practical criticism and theory? These questions (which appear to have framed themselves in Miller's seductive style) lead us to the first of the texts I want to read beside Miller's essay on "The Rock." This is "Theory and Practice: Response to Vincent Leitch," Miller's reply to the 1980 essay cited earlier. Miller's (mild) objection to Leitch's account of his criticism is that the general formulations of deconstruction that Leitch has abstracted from "the context of the practical interpretation which fathered them" has tended to give them "a higher level of universality than they have in the original." Miller argues that seeing a concept clearly "cannot occur as abstract theory but only by way of reflection about concrete acts of interpreting particular works." Leitch "should perhaps have said something about the particular readings that are associated with the general statements he cites." And "he might have raised the question of the relation between the two,"[6] that is, between the particular reading and the general theory.

What Miller here contends Leitch has left undone is what I wish to pursue. I want to examine the relation between Miller's form of deconstructive criticism and his concrete act of interpreting "The Rock." I accept, at least provisionally, his premise that the "test of the efficacity, if not of the 'validity,' of a given theory is the persuasiveness of the readings it enables." There is, however, one distinction between theory and practice in his essay that, if correct, will tend to make the kind of examination I propose, the analysis of a particular and unique act of reading, more difficult. Miller argues that "a theory is easier to refute or to dismiss than is a reading," and this is because "a reading can only be successfully opposed by another reading," which involves "returning to the text in question and working back through it."[7]

Miller's limiting of the authority of any critique of his own reading—it would be simply another reading and necessarily a misreading—is only one of a number of defenses that have rendered deconstructive criticism particularly resistant to attack. And to question Miller's methodology or the cogency of a particular reading, as I want to do here, is to risk what could be called (after one of the first to experience it) the Abrams Effect. This is the recognition that *any* argument against a deconstructive reading—the basis or logic of the argument being largely irrelevant—may be dismantled by the rhetoric of deconstruction, which has been formulated, not incidentally, to do just that, to neutralize the logic of any form of extended statement.[8] It is deconstruction's good fortune, and perhaps the secret of whatever longevity it has enjoyed, that its resourceful rhetoric, its method of reading literary and philosophical texts, works equally well against the attacks of its opponents.

I want to argue that Miller misreads "The Rock," and he would no doubt agree, since all readings are in his view necessarily misreadings. I must therefore scrutinize the standards and concepts implied in his actual practice, and what I will attempt to show is that among these is the notion of misreading in the traditional sense of an unnecessary and correctable misreading. In questioning Miller's interpretation of Stevens' "The Rock," I want to be able to make the same distinctions among different kinds of misreading that Miller himself finds it necessary to make. It is evident that critics like Miller and Bloom, who assume that all reading is misreading, find themselves in situations in which their official conceptions of misreading prove insufficient or incoherent. Miller borrows, apparently from Bloom, a distinction between strong and weak misreadings as a way out of his quandary, but this brings with it some confusion, for Miller's strong misreading is clearly not the same as Bloom's, lacking (at least in theory) its Freudian willfulness.[9]

Although the notion of a weak misreading does not always mean the same thing for Bloom, one of its functions is to enable him to say that someone is clearly mistaken and can be shown to be so, as in this comment on an allusion to Shelley in a passage from Stevens' poem "Mr. Burnshaw and the Statue": "Critics have misread this, weakly, as an attack upon Shelley, which the context alone would reveal to be unlikely, and which Stevens, in a letter, clearly disowns, in a strong tribute to the harmonious skeptic among his Romantic precursors."[10] That is, these critics' misreadings are neither necessary nor strong (willful), and their mistaken ideas could be corrected by a better understanding of the context in which the Shelley allusion occurs and by a reading of Stevens' letter, which Bloom proceeds to cite. For Bloom, then, *all* reading is misreading and *some* reading is misreading in yet another sense, and he finds it necessary to draw distinctions. This is a dilemma that Miller also faces, and the text that reveals it most forcefully is "Deconstructing the Deconstructers," his 1975 *Diacritics* review of Joseph Riddel's reading of *The Inverted Bell*, a deconstruction of William Carlos Williams' poetics.

Miller uses the review, which preceded the Stevens essay by a year, as an occasion for clarifying the tenets of deconstruction as he sees them, which necessarily involves showing how Riddel's version of deconstruction is mistaken. He recognizes immediately that his central concept of misreading makes this task more difficult. His discomfort can be read in his phrasing of his contentions as questions and his final resort to Bloom's strong and weak misreadings:

> First there is the question of Riddel's reading of Heidegger and Derrida. Has he got them right? What would it mean to "get them right?" If all interpretation is misinterpretation, this would be as true of Riddel's reading of Heidegger as of Wordsworth's reading of Milton. Does the necessity of misreading mean the same thing in each case? Then there is the question of Riddel's reading of Williams. Has he got Williams right? Even if the law of misreading applies here also, there are obviously strong and weak misreadings, more or less vital ones.[11]

Miller wishes to say that Riddel's reading does not get Heidegger, Derrida, and Williams "right," while admitting that no reading could possibly get them right. His means of escaping his dilemma are to suggest that misreading does not mean the same thing in each case and to find equivocal terms—"vital" and "coherent" are examples—with which to question the competency of Riddel's reading.

"Is Riddel's own critical language coherent? Does he say the same thing from one end of his book to the other?"[12] Miller asks, forgetting for a moment his own view that no text is coherent, that no book is able to say the same thing from one end to the other. Miller's implication is that Riddel's critical language is not coherent and that his deconstructive reading misinterprets Heidegger, Derrida, and Williams. The question is whether these are necessary misreadings, inherent in the nature of all reading, or misreadings that may be traced to the competency of the reader. For Miller's own review to escape incoherence (chiding a fellow critic for what is inescapable in their joint enterprise), they must fall into the second category.

This conclusion—that some misreadings may be attributed to the incompetency of the reader—is reinforced by Miller's intimation (again by way of a question) that Riddel is simply confused: "Is he confused in a way which might have been clarified, or is there some necessity in the deconstructive enterprise which means that it is always open in its turn to desconstruction [*sic*]?" The answer is the former: "His book would have been clarified if he had remained more faithful to his intermittent insight into the difference between Heidegger and Derrida," and "he would have been aided by a more elaborate rhetorical theory and by a more discriminating attention to the play of figures in his authors." These are obviously correctable mistakes, as is Riddel's major failure: "Perhaps the most difficulty is caused in Riddel's book, however, by his failure to recognize consistently the necessary heterogeneity of any text." It is *Riddel's* failure, then, that has produced his misreadings and not the contradictions in the texts he reads. "The clearer deconstructions are those which are most sensitive to the complexities of figure, to that range of different figures which current rhetoric is recovering as a tool of literary analysis." Riddel's misreadings are the result of his not understanding this: "Riddel for the most part does not face explicitly the heterogeneity of Williams or of the other authors he discusses. The result is that he contradicts himself, rather than recognizing fully the contradictions in the texts he discusses."[13]

These are the distinctions that "Deconstructing the Deconstructers" struggles to express without unmasking its own contradictions. Yet I am willing to accept Miller's distinctions between forms of misreading, contradictions included, as a means of approaching his reading of "The Rock." I mean to show that there are at least two kinds of misreading present in his essay, but that his "weak" misreadings—those that may be attributed to the lack of competency of the reading rather than contradictions in the text—are primarily responsible for the essay's essential incoherence. As he says of Riddel, even if the general law of misreading applies here, there are strong and weak critical misreadings, the latter consisting of confusions that might be "clarified," that reside in the critic's commentary as the result of a failure of recognition or understanding, although, in this instance, not independent of the general theory that sanctions them.

A feature of Miller's method of reading, as is well known, is to direct attention to one or more crucial passages in a text (as opposed to the text as a whole), sometimes passages of only a few lines, which signal an impasse or contradiction or a moment of undecidability. "Stevens' Rock and Criticism as Cure" begins with one such passage from "The Rock" (*CP* 525):

> It is not enough to cover the rock with leaves.
> We must be cured of it by a cure of the ground
> Or a cure of ourselves, that is equal to a cure
>
> Of the ground, a cure beyond forgetfulness.

"A 'cure of the ground'? What can this mean?" Miller asks, and begins his play with the many senses of the word "cure," tracing its etymology and applying its contradictory meanings to the passage at hand, as he would manipulate "host" and "parasite" in his MLA paper "The Critic as Host" a few months later. He concludes, "The multiple meanings of the word 'cure,' like the meanings of all the key words and figures in 'The Rock,' are incompatible, irreconcilable. They may not be organized into a logical or dialectical structure but remain stubbornly heterogeneous." The phrase "a cure of the ground" announces a moment of the poem's unreadability, and subsequent passages that contain the word "cure" are also contaminated by it: "The meaning of the passages in 'The Rock' turning on the word 'cure' oscillates painfully within the reader's mind. However hard he tries to fix the word in a single sense it remains indeterminable, uncannily resisting his attempts to end the movement." Miller is a careful reader and much of what he says about Stevens' poem is persuasive, but his interpretation of what is for him its key passage is so seriously flawed that it undermines the entire reading and the more general observations about deconstructive criticism that depend on it. (The phrase "a cure of the ground," as Miller understands its use in the poem, becomes a key figure in the second part of the essay, which departs from the poem to discuss the principles of deconstructive criticism.) I will concentrate my reading on that essential portion of the essay that deals with Stevens' "cure of the ground" since, as Bloom observes, "the notion of 'cure' is central to [Miller's] reading."[14]

"The Rock" is at least in part a poem about its speaker's sense of nothingness or meaninglessness and his attempt to be cured of it. The figure of the bare rock is associated with nothingness, and the cure that the poem speaks of is pictured either as covering the rock with vegetation, concealing the nothingness (although that is "not enough"), or making "meanings of the rock" so that "its barrenness ... exists no more." The first of the poem's three sections,[15] "Seventy Years Later," introduces the concept of nothingness as an act of forgetting the past. To the seventy-year-old speaker, incidents from the past have taken on a sense of absurdity, as if they never existed, were merely figments of someone's (or something's) imagination. "It is an illusion that we were ever alive," he begins, "Lived in the houses of mothers, arranged ourselves / By our own motion in a freedom of air." But it is not simply that they *no longer* seem real; their unreality is such as to suggest that they *never* existed. "The lives these lived in the mind are at an end," he says, initiating a conventional interpretation of the remoteness of the past, but then correcting himself: "They never were." It is the unconventional sense of the past as never existing that inserts the concept of nothingness into the poem: "The sounds of the guitar / Were not and are not. Absurd. The words spoken / Were not and are not. It is not to be believed."

Miller's paraphrase of this first section is relatively straightforward and unproblematic. The necessity of misreading is an issue for him only at certain points in the text. At other points he does not appear to question his ability to "'say the same thing' as the poetic texts say." "The first six stanzas of 'Seventy Years Later,'" he writes, "record a radical act of forgetting," which "annihilates everything that seemed most vital in the poet's past, most solidly grounded." He also paraphrases straightforwardly Stevens' conceit of nothingness as containing a "métier," a vocation or "assumption" by which the illusion of the past has been produced, but he does not recognize the relation between the notion of the speaker's past as the invention of a "fantastic consciousness" and the poem's "cure of the ground." The first section, that is, concludes with the fiction that appears with increasing frequency in Stevens' later poems. Although Miller argues that "'rock,' 'ground,' and even 'forgetfulness' readers of Stevens will be able to interpret from other poems by him,"[16] his own interpretation limits this principle of intratextual reading to particular words rather than larger themes or concepts.

As I have underscored in earlier chapters, "The Auroras of Autumn" (*CP* 411) toys with the notion that we and our world are the thoughts of a cosmic imagination "which in the midst of summer stops to imagine winter," and I have argued that a number of the poems of *The Rock* deal with similar conceptions, including, most notably, "The Plain Sense of Things," "Looking Across the Fields and Watching the Birds Fly," "The World as Meditation," and "Final Soliloquy of the Interior Paramour." In "The Rock" the speaker and the incidents of his past are also seen as the inventions of an external consciousness seeking its own happiness:

> The meeting at noon at the edge of the field seems like
>
> An invention, an embrace between one desperate clod
> And another in a fantastic consciousness,
> In a queer assertion of humanity:
>
> A theorem proposed between the two—
> Two figures in a nature of the sun,
> In the sun's design of its own happiness,
>
> As if nothingness contained a métier,
> A vital assumption. . . .

To think of oneself as an "invention," a "theorem," or an "assumption" is of course to be reduced to the content of a mind or imagination, to become an idea, and the reduction is heightened by the suggestion that the idea the speaker constitutes is itself an illusion, something created to cover an essential emptiness. The "vital assumption" contained in nothingness is "an illusion so desired / That the green leaves came and covered the high rock, / That the lilacs came and bloomed, like a blindness cleaned. . . ."

The conceit of "Seventy Years Later," which will be central to the following section (and to Miller's impasse, although he apparently does not recognize it), is that the natural world, including the speaker, is an illusion created from the nothingness that underlies it, and that its purpose is to cover over nothingness. Or to shift the metaphor and borrow the key term from the following section, if nothingness is a kind of blindness, then the invented natural world is sight, "curing" blindness. As the poem puts it, the métier or assumption contained in nothingness "was satisfied, / In a birth of sight." And if the natural world is thought of as a fiction, an invention or illusion, then its inventor may be thought of as a kind of artist or poet, as in "Long and Sluggish Lines" (*CP* 522), where the "pre-history of February" is "The life of the poem in the mind [that] has not yet begun." This implied parallel between the natural world and the poem is also central to Miller's key passage in part two of the poem, which compares the cure offered by the poem with nature's cure, the leaves. The leaves and lilacs are synecdochic figures for the whole of the natural world, for life itself, the entire "gross universe." The audacious premise of "The Rock" is that the "particular[s] of being" represent an attempted "cure" offered by some activity contained in the nothingness on which they rest: "The blooming and the musk / Were being alive, an incessant being alive, / A particular of being, that gross universe."

Miller offers this passage as one example of the poem's unreadability, and his discussion of it is an example of a "clear" or strong as opposed to a weak misreading, since it points to a difficulty in the text rather than creating one in the commentary. He notes that the sequence of phrases in apposition, as here, creates problems in interpretation, since "the relation among the elements in such a series is undecidable, abyssed." In the passage above, "The phrase 'that gross universe' is placed in apposition with the subsidiary word 'being' in the phrase before, rather than with the apparently parallel word 'particular,'" and the "sequence plays with various incongruent senses and grammatical functions of the word 'being.'"[17] It is true that the final phrase "that gross universe" is not precisely parallel, but the progression of the sequence of phrases appears to be functional, especially when read in its larger context. The passage in which it appears begins with particular leaves and lilacs and ends with the entire visible universe as an attempted remedy for nothingness's blindness, "gross" here both in the sense of "glaringly noticeable" and "growing or spreading with excessive luxuriance." "Seventy Years Later" thus ends with the "gross" universe as one instance of the attempt to overcome the sense of nothingness, in effect the non-human world's own attempt; the second section, "The Poem as Icon," deals with an example of a parallel human attempt, the poem.

The poem is an icon because its attempt to cover the barrenness of the rock or otherwise cure us of its nothingness resembles nature's cure, so the poem is an image or a figure for the natural process described in the first section. There are thus two cures spoken of in the second section, a "cure of the ground" (the "natural" cure described in the first section) and a "cure of ourselves," of which the poem is the prime instance. "The Poem as Icon" is concerned with the particular value of the poem as a cure of nothingness, its superiority to the simple covering of the rock with leaves. It is, in effect, a justification of poetry as a source of meaning. The poem does more than hide the rock; it "makes meanings of the rock, / Of such mixed motion and such imagery / That its barrenness becomes a thousand things / And so exists no more."

We are now in a position to reread Miller's crucial passage and his weak misreading of it. The passage opens the second section and obviously refers back to the conclusion of the first, nature's covering of the rock with leaves and lilacs. The second section says that this is not enough in itself (as was demonstrated by the speaker's forgetfulness, his loss of the meaning of his past). The cure he seeks is "beyond forgetfulness":

> It is not enough to cover the rock with leaves.
> We must be cured of it by a cure of the ground
> Or a cure of ourselves, that is equal to a cure
>
> Of the ground, a cure beyond forgetfulness.

Miller's misreading of this key passage differs from his strong misreading of the sequence of phrases in apposition cited above, since that reading supposedly extends an impasse in the text. This misreading simply mistakes Stevens' use of a preposition.

The title of Richard Hull's 1935 novel *The Murder of My Aunt* plays on the reader's tendency to interpret "of" in such a way as to make the aunt the victim of the murder. This impression is reinforced by the fact that the story is told from the point of view of the nephew who plots against her. But the novel proper ends prior to the murder, and the last section, called "Postscript," picks up the story from the point of view of the aunt, who turns out to be the murderer of the nephew, as the title had informed us all along if we had been alert to its implications. The last paragraph of the novel is this, in the aunt's words:

> I have now only to add a title to these notes, and the one I have chosen perhaps needs a word of explanation. Well, "of" can be possessive, can't it? Can mean "of or belonging to."[18]

The primary sense of the preposition in Stevens' "cure of the ground" and "cure of ourselves" is one that Miller, like the hypothetical reader of *The Murder of My Aunt*, does not consider. It is, I am arguing, the cure "of or belonging to" the ground and the cure "of or belonging to" ourselves. This interpretation is suggested by the context alone, but it is reinforced by Stevens' use of the construction "cure of" in his "Adagia"—"Poetry is a cure of the mind" (*OP* 201). Miller cites this as one of Stevens' few uses of "cure," but he does not see its implication for his reading of "The Rock."

As Stevens makes clear in poems such as "Man and Bottle" (*CP* 238) and "Of Modern Poetry" (*CP* 239), "of the mind" in the phrase above also uses "of" as a possessive to mean "belonging to." In "Man and Bottle" poetry is "of the mind" because it is "A manner of thinking, a mode / Of destroying, as the mind destroys. . . ." In "Of Modern Poetry" the poem is a mental act. It begins, "The poem of the mind in the act of finding / What will suffice," and ends, "The poem of the act of the mind." Since the poem is defined as an "act of the mind," the "Adagia" maxim surely does not say that the poem cures the mind, but that it is the cure "of or belonging to" the mind. Similarly, the "cure of ourselves" is the cure we offer, just as the "cure of the ground" is the cure offered by the ground.

Miller's failure to consider this possibility—he does not argue that the preposition is ambiguous—makes nonsense of much of his reading as he strains to find ways that the ground can be cured. Here is a representative selection of his reading of a "cure of the ground," which goes on for several pages:

> The cure of the ground would be a caring for the ground, a securing of it, making it solid, as one cures a fiberglass hull by drying it carefully. At the same time the cure of the ground must be an effacing of it, making it vanish as a medicine cures a man of a disease by taking it away, making him sound again, or as an infatuated man is cured of a dangerous illusion. "Cure" comes from Latin *cura*, care, as in "curate" or "a cure of souls." The word "scour," which I used above, has the same root. A cure of the ground would scour it clean, revealing the bedrock beneath. Such a curing would be at the same time—according to an obsolete meaning of the word, with a different root, Middle English *cuuve*, cover, conceal, protect—a caring for the ground by hiding it.[19]

But of course if the preposition in "cure of the ground" is possessive, then Miller's pages of etymologies—his scouring, effacing, concealing, protecting, and securing—as well as his conclusion that "cure of the ground" here is unreadable for the reasons that he offers, are fatally undermined.

What is the poem's context for "cure"? Are the passages that contain the word in fact unreadable? I want to paraphrase this portion of the poem in as direct and elementary a manner as possible. The key passage in which the word occurs begins by referring back to the fiction of the first section, the fantastic consciousness that produces "an illusion so desired / That the green leaves came and covered the high rock." The opening passage of "The Poem as Icon" says that "It is not enough to cover the rock with leaves," that is, simply to hide it. We must be "cured of it," of the rock, of the barrenness it represents, but by what? By a cure of the ground, first of all, but what might that be? The ground or the earth is the source of the leaves that cover the rock, but that covering in itself does not constitute a cure. Yet, the poem says, the leaves may be the beginning of a cure of the ground:

> And yet the leaves, if they broke into bud,
> If they broke into bloom, if they bore fruit,
>
> And if we ate the incipient colorings
> Of their fresh culls might be a cure of the ground.

In "Seventy Years Later" the leaves are associated with "being alive" or "particular[s] of being." Now the speaker says that if these particulars of being are more than a cover for the rock but help to nourish our lives, they might constitute a cure of the ground. To phrase it differently, if the particular experiences of living in the world are fruitful and if we "feast" on life—if we devour it so that it becomes a part of us—this could be seen as a cure of nothingness or meaninglessness offered by the earth, as opposed to a cure that *we* contrive, the other possible cure the poem considers. "To eat the fruit would be to possess the whole and so to cure the ground," Miller writes. "It would be to understand it, in the etymological sense of reaching the base and standing there, in a 'final found,' with a multiple pun on 'found' as discover, invention, and foundation."[20] This approaches nonsense and does not state a relationship between eating the fruit and curing the ground. It is difficult to think of any sense in which the eating of fruit constitutes a curing of the ground that produced it, and it is scarcely surprising that Miller's weak misreading produces an impasse, a condition of what he names unreadability.

But what of the context of a "cure of ourselves"? Here the preposition is more ambiguous, but the primary sense is still the cure "of or belonging to" ourselves rather than "curing ourselves." We are to be cured *of* something by either "a cure of the ground" or "a cure of ourselves" that must be at least "equal to a cure / Of the ground." If we read the passage from Miller's perspective then its sense is "we must be cured of something by being cured," which appears redundant. What the passage says is rather that the cure that comes from ourselves must be equal to the cure that comes from the ground, or, to put it in Stevens' more habitual terms, the human imagination must be equal to reality[21]—although reality here is figured, paradoxically, as the creation of a non-human imagination.

The cure that comes from ourselves, from the human imagination, is the "fiction of the leaves," which is the "icon of the poem." The poem's fictional leaves are the human equivalent of the natural world's vegetation (which the poem depicts as a non-human fiction); both cover the bare rock of nothingness. The fictional leaves of the poem, however, have the advantage that "They bud and bloom and bear their fruit *without change*" (my emphasis). They are therefore in at least one sense "beyond forgetfulness." They are also "more than leaves that cover the barren rock," since the poem "makes meanings of the rock"—human meanings—in a manner that the natural cure cannot achieve. Miller says, oddly, "The cure of the ground proposed in the poem is the poem itself," but the poem's distinction between the ground's cure and our cure—the poem—is emphatic. Near the end of "The Poem as Icon" is a sentence that should have alerted Miller to his erroneous reading of the preposition: "This is the cure / Of leaves and of the ground and of ourselves." The addition of leaves to the equation—the leaves are clearly one source of the cure, not something to be cured—and the parallel construction of the three phrases make more obvious than earlier passages that "of" here is possessive, and consequently that a great deal of what Miller says about the poem is based on a misreading that belongs to his commentary and not to the text. This is not to say that my reading of "The Rock" is the "correct" reading— that I know what the poem means and Miller does not—or even that there could be a definitive reading of the poem. I am rather questioning the persuasiveness of Miller's reading in the only manner he thinks possible: "a reading can only be successfully opposed by another reading."[22] And my further argument, as a footnote in the history of deconstructive criticism, is that one of the seminal essays of the movement is based on what is very nearly a howler.

What is most significant about Miller's apparently simple misunderstanding of a preposition is that it infects almost every aspect of the essay, including its very title. Because he takes Stevens' "cure of the ground" to mean "curing the ground," the "Criticism as Cure" of his title incorporates that erroneous reading when criticism becomes, later in the essay, a "cure of the ground." "The poem itself rises as an icon which is the equivalent of the leaves, blossom, and fruit and so cures the ground," Miller writes, and in the second part of the essay (which uses the terms of his misreading to characterize deconstruction) he argues that "criticism is a continuation of that activity of the poem":

> If the poem is a cure of the ground which never succeeds, criticism is a yielding to the temptation to try once more for the "cure beyond forgetfulness," and then once more, and once beyond that, in an ever-renewed, ever-unsuccessful attempt to "get it right," to name things by their right names. . . . The critical text prolongs, extends, reveals, covers, in short, cures, the literary text in the same way that the literary text attempts to cure the ground.[23]

But of course the assertion that the literary text attempts to cure the ground (whatever that might mean) is not, as I have tried to show, sanctioned by Stevens' use of these terms, and Miller's use of "cure" and "ground" throughout part two of his essay is undermined by his misunderstanding of what they imply in the poem.

Unfortunately for the argument of the second half of the essay, they are the two key terms. "If poetry is the impossible possible cure of the ground," he writes, establishing his central figure, "criticism is the impossible possible cure of literature." Criticism becomes a cure of the ground in various senses: "The 'deconstruction' which the text performs on itself and which the critic repeats is not of the superstructure of the work but of the ground on which it stands."

What he calls the Socratic or scientific criticism that stands opposed to deconstruction would try to cure the ground in a different way; it "would be not only a penetration of the ground but also its correction, its straightening out." Deconstruction, on the other hand, "annihilates the ground on which the building stands by showing that the text has already annihilated that ground, knowingly or unknowingly." "Ground" becomes increasingly important as the essay progresses. The text's "apparently solid ground is no rock but thin air." The criticism of de Man, Bloom, Hartman, and Derrida "is an interrogation of the ground of literature, not just of its intrinsic structure." The concluding sentence of the essay spells out clearly, in the task Miller sets for criticism, just why criticism is for him a cure of the ground and why his misreading of "The Rock" has seized on that phrase: "The task of criticism in the immediate future should be the further exploration, as much by practical essays of interpretation as by theoretical speculation, of this coming and going in quest and in questioning of the ground."[24]

The ground that serves as the foundation for Miller's own exploration, I have argued, turns out to be thin air; but is this argument in itself merely a confirmation of deconstruction's premise that all reading is misreading? That might indeed be the case if the term "misreading" always referred to the same activity and if each particular instance of misreading could be shown to be *necessary*. Miller's motive in reading "The Rock" is of course to demonstrate that the misreading *is* a necessary one, an acknowledgment of the heterogeneity of the poem and in particular of its key phrase, "cure of the ground." Whether or not his misreading of "The Rock" is an instance of the necessity of misreading thus depends in part on the persuasiveness of my own reading of Stevens' "cure of the ground" and the argument, based on it, that the context of the poem and the larger context of Stevens' writings are sufficient to correct his misreading.

Even the most persuasive reading of "The Rock" cannot in itself invalidate the claim that all reading is, in some sense, misreading (misreading perhaps as simply the absence of a definitive interpretation),[25] but it can raise questions about Miller's own practice of misreading and its relation to the theory that sanctions it. Miller writes, "The only way persuasively to challenge deconstructionist readings . . . would not be to construct an alternative theory but to show the inadequacy of the particular readings associated inextricably with whatever is 'theoretical' in such work."[26] I have attempted to show the inadequacy of Miller's reading of "The Rock," but is its inadequacy tied to his theory? It is, it seems to me, in one obvious sense. Miller's theory that all texts are unreadable, that all texts contain the kind of incoherence exemplified by "The Rock"'s "cure of the ground," leads to a practice that oddly and perversely rewards the reading that fails to make connections, is blind to the relation between a particular passage and a larger context, confuses the function of grammatical units, or distorts a text in its paraphrase to produce incoherence. Had Miller not mistaken the use of a preposition in "The Rock," or had he not failed to see the implications of the "Adagia" maxim "Poetry is a cure of the mind" or the implications of other themes and fictions in *The Rock* as a whole—the fiction of a "fantastic consciousness," for example, which cures the barrenness of the rock for "its own happiness"—Stevens' phrase "cure of the ground" would have been of much less value to his essay. Indeed, the essay might never have been written.

"When we are confronted with any manifestation which some one has permitted us to see," Nietzsche writes in *The Dawn of Day,* "we may ask: what is it meant to conceal? What is it meant to draw our attention from?" Another feature of Miller's practice of misreading is his willingness to permit us to see that he has done violence to the text under examination. In an essay on *Heart of Darkness,* for example, he speaks at the end of his "own complicity" in obscuring the meaning of the novel. He has "attempted to perform an act of generic classification, with all the covert violence and unreason of that act"; he is "guilty . . . of covering over while claiming to illuminate." He calls attention to his misreading, however, only on the basis that it is a universal condition—the necessity of all texts, including his own, to be misunderstood. The activity of deconstruction, he notes in the essay on "The Rock," can be done "only in such a way as to be misunderstood in its turn, like the work itself, so that it has to be done over, and then again." The effect of such an emphasis on general misreading is to draw our attention from the details of a particular misreading, as in the case of Miller's reading of "The Rock," to conceal the fact that each particular misreading is, like this one, personal and eccentric, its form not the inevitable result of some general condition of reading. Miller holds that "the particular way in which a given work is unreadable may be exactly specified," and it is this principle as it applies to "The Rock" that can be shown to be mistaken, since it assumes that the critic is pointing to an incoherence in the text and not creating one by an inadequate reading. Moreover, to contend that the way in which a given text is unreadable may be "exactly specified" comes dangerously near the principle of a "definitive" misreading. Robert Markley, who argues that Miller's reading of "The Rock" is a manifestation of a "style" and not a "system of ideas," speaks of the language of the essay as "deliberately hypnotic" and labels its rhetoric as "incantatory."[27] The ability of Miller's rhetoric of misreading to distract us from the text under examination, to direct our attention away from the basis of the interpretation being offered, may be one explanation for the fact that in the decades since "Stevens' Rock and Criticism as Cure" appeared, no one has pointed out just how badly it distorts Stevens' poem in the service of the theory it sought to institute.

6 / Conclusion:
After the *Collected Poems*

A book that contains everything that one has done in a lifetime does not reassure one. Then, the fact that I am 75 begins to seem like the most serious thing that has ever happened to me.

—STEVENS, *Letters*

THE LAST POEMS STEVENS WROTE, in 1954 and 1955, after the *Collected Poems* had been compiled,[1] suggest the direction a new volume might have taken had he lived to complete it. As a group they are less intimate and less accessible than the poems of *The Rock,* although there are exceptions—"As You Leave the Room," for one. In their abstraction some of them surpass even the most difficult of the poems of *The Auroras of Autumn.* Others—"Of Mere Being" is the chief example—impede access because they attempt to express what appears inexpressible, unthinkable, or, as the poem has it, what is "Beyond the last thought." In conjunction with their difficulty, their exclusion from the *Collected Poems* has resulted in their being largely unread, reduced to passing references. With the exception of the two poems mentioned above and perhaps "The Sail of Ulysses," they have not been subjected to the normally fruitful process of critical debate.

"The Sail of Ulysses" (*OP* 126), written for Columbia's bicentennial commencement and delivered as the Phi Beta Kappa poem at the end of May 1954, is the most ambitious of the uncollected poems and the one that most disappointed Stevens himself. A few days after he read it, he wrote to the poet and critic Babette Deutsch that he would "certainly never use it in its present form nor allow anyone to see a copy of it"; according to Holly Stevens, he refused to furnish copies to the Columbia faculty who wrote requesting them (*Letters* 834 n. 6). "Perhaps I shan't throw it away," he told Deutsch, adding, "I am going to do a little more work on it and then, if I like it, I may at least keep it without any thought of doing anything with it" (*Letters* 834, 835). What he salvaged from its 176 lines was a twenty-four-line poem, "Presence of an External Master of Knowledge," and the title for "A Child Asleep in Its Own Life." Four months after the bicentennial celebration, he wrote to the Columbia professor Horace Taylor, "What there is left of *The Sail of Ulysses* which I read before Phi Beta Kappa last spring has just appeared in a supplement to the London Times Literary Section devoted to American literature. The title has been changed to *Presence of an External Master of Knowledge.*" He also told Taylor, "The poem in the Times does not represent the substance of the original poem. It is merely one aspect of it which I liked" (*Letters* 834–35 n. 6).

Stevens laid some of the blame for the poem's failure on Taylor, with whom he had negotiated about its theme. He told Deutsch, "Ordinarily, a Phi Beta Kappa poet can choose his own subject" (as had been the case when Stevens read "Description without Place" as the Phi Beta Kappa poem at Harvard a decade earlier). On this occasion, however, "I was asked to write a poem which would have to do with one aspect of the birthday theme." When he responded that this would create a difficulty, he was told that "it would be all right if I would merely use some of the words" (*Letters* 835), that is, the words associated with the bicentennial theme—as reported by Alan Filreis, "Man's Right to Knowledge and the Free Use Thereof." He was unhappy with the poem not because "knowledge is not a good subject for a poem but because, coupled with birthdays and commencements, it becomes a force of intolerable generalities." A public poem on "Man's Right to Knowledge and the Free Use Thereof" for so unpublic a poet as Stevens obviously presented difficulties. "One of the great difficulties," he concluded, "was to read so abstract a poem in such a way as not to create confusion. I don't think that I succeeded" (*Letters* 835). Many of its readers would no doubt agree with Stevens' judgment, and one indication of that is the absence of any sustained or engaging criticism on the poem itself (as opposed to its occasion, which Filreis has engagingly examined in some detail). It is frequently mentioned, sometimes in connection with Stevens' Penelope poem, "The World as Meditation," but readers have had difficulty finding anything to say about it. In the density of its abstractions it rivals "The Owl in the Sarcophagus," a poem that Harold Bloom characterizes as "not wholly available to even the most prolonged and loving of readings."[2]

Filreis, who has a more favorable opinion of the poem than most readers, reports that Stevens told Taylor sometime after the reading that he "deliberately wrote an abstract poem." Filreis believes that Stevens is somewhat disingenuous in his protests to Deutsch about his lack of freedom in selecting a subject (a deeply ironic situation, in view of the bicentennial's theme). It is true that the bicentennial committee suggested to Stevens a poem in which he would incorporate such expressions as *right, knowledge,* and *freedom,* but Filreis points out that Stevens did more than simply use some of the words of the bicentennial theme. "In point of fact," he writes, "[Stevens] aimed so strategically at topicality, at incorporating the words in the thematic phrase and meeting the demands of the public genre, that that and nothing else was why the result seemed later, even to him, a perfect 'confusion.'"[3] This is not quite the case, since there is something else that is in part responsible for the poem's confusion, as I want to argue shortly, but Filreis is correct in emphasizing the degree to which "The Sail of Ulysses" tackles the bicentennial theme of knowledge head-on, if not perhaps in the spirit suggested by the university's slogan.

And indeed the poem's confusion may be greater for a reader today than it was for its original audience, which heard it as a public declaration on "Man's Right to Knowledge," in which variations on the word *knowledge* spring up frequently. The poem, as Stevens recognized, speaks in generalities—"the right to know / And the right to be are one"; "How then shall the mind be less than free / Since only to know is to be free"—which are puzzling for present-day readers because they seem to come from nowhere. They lack the context that would make them compelling or even intelligible. Filreis has attempted to supply a context by pointing out the extent to which "the right to know" and "the right to be" were significant issues in May 1954, both at Columbia and nationally:

> The heated debate about "the right to know," the terms of which were largely set by [Joseph] McCarthy and his adherents, had preoccupied Columbia for months before Wallace Stevens arrived on the scene; the right to be and the right to know seemed sadly irreconcilable in ways the Columbia audience would have understood perfectly after a winter and spring of national events—the army-McCarthy hearings and a new wave of academic dismissals—had created the context for widely publicized bicentennial events that made the paradox distinct. When Stevens decided it would be one of the tasks of his poem to attempt at least a provisional reconciliation of contending concepts of rights, he was advancing a position in an important public argument—an argument he had doubtless been hearing.

This ideological context dispels some of the confusion of "The Sail of Ulysses," or at least of its first section, which now becomes a treatise on Ulysses' opening words: "'As I know, I am and have / The right to be.'" We now understand why, as Filreis also points out, the word *right*, used only four times in Stevens' previous poems, is used fourteen times in this one, and why some form of *knowledge* or *know* appears twenty-three times. It is a poem, in the view of Filreis, which takes up a current debate between competing rights, the conservative right to know versus the liberal right to "be," that is, to live freely as one chooses. Its solution appears to be that there is no competition between these rights, since "the right to know and the right to be could be understood as one."[4]

Or so Filreis reads it, and that certainly is the argument of the poem's first section. After a six-line prologue that introduces Ulysses as the "Symbol of the seeker," the remainder of the poem, with the exception of a six-line coda, is comprised of Ulysses' soliloquy. He is not the adventurous Ulysses of Homer but a meditative Ulysses, perhaps a younger version of Tennyson's more thoughtful Ulysses, especially in his "desire / To follow knowledge like a sinking star, / Beyond the utmost bound of human thought." He is introduced "Guiding his boat / Under the middle stars," and he exits somewhat mysteriously "As if another sail went on / Straight forwardly through another night / And clumped stars dangled all the way." His soliloquy begins rather abruptly with an "if . . . then" argument that equates knowledge and life:

> "If knowledge and the thing known are one
> So that to know a man is to be
> That man, to know a place is to be
> That place, and it seems to come to that;
> And if one's sense of a single spot
> Is what one knows of the universe,
> Then knowledge is the only life,
> The only sun of the only day,
> The only access to true ease,
> The deep comfort of the world and fate."

If the poem were to be primarily an examination of the relations of the right to know and the right to be, as Filreis believes, then this would be a fitting conclusion, but, curiously, it is where it begins the first of its eight cantos. The poem as a whole does not appear to be an examination of the claims of competing rights; rather it begins with the assumption that knowing and being are, in some sense not fully evident, the same and proceeds to other epistemological (rather than political) issues that follow from this assumption. And what of the assumption itself? Is it true that "to know a place is to be / That place"? What does it mean to *be a place*? In what sense could one "be / That man" simply by knowing him? It is the use of the concept of being that creates the difficulty. Is this nonsense, or does Stevens have ulterior motives in his use of Columbia's bicentennial language? What is it that he wishes to say, in this abstract and willfully obscure poem, about knowledge and being?

What especially interests Stevens here about these concepts are two ideas that run throughout the poems of *The Rock* and show up also in the short poem he made from "The Sail of Ulysses"—first, the relationship between a certain kind of knowing and need or destitution and, secondly and more importantly, the kind of knowledge that would indeed be the equivalent of being—that of an external master of knowledge. Stevens told Horace Taylor that "Presence of an External Master of Knowledge," represented "one aspect of ["The Sail of Ulysses"] which I liked," and its title makes clear what aspect that is. "The Sail of Ulysses" develops abstractly and obscurely the intimations of Penelope in "The World as Meditation" and the irrational thought of the Stevens persona in "Final Soliloquy of the Interior Paramour," both of whom in their loneliness or need feel the presence of an external master of knowledge. As the latter poem has it, "We feel the obscurity of an order, a whole, / A knowledge, that which arranged the rendezvous / Within its vital boundary, in the mind" (*CP* 524).

"The Sail of Ulysses" first states a relation between loneliness and knowledge in a manner that is puzzling. The second canto begins with Ulysses saying,

> "There is a human loneliness,
> A part of space and solitude,
> In which knowledge cannot be denied,
> In which nothing of knowledge fails,
> The luminous companion, the hand,
> The fortifying arm, the profound
> Response, the completely answering voice,
> That which is more than anything else
> The right within us and about us,
> Joined, the triumphant vigor, felt. . . ."

This is dense to the point of being almost unreadable. Does it say that a condition of loneliness is somehow a more fruitful source of knowledge than other states? If so, why would that be true? "Why, after all, could the condition 'In which knowledge cannot be denied' not be characterized without reference to solitude?" Mark Halliday asks. "Why indeed could the condition not be imagined as in some way a social condition?"[5] That question is answered in the poem's final section, in Ulysses' meditation on knowledge and deprivation. But other questions are raised here. In what sense is knowledge now the "luminous companion" or the "completely answering voice," and what is it that is joined at the conclusion of the passage? In his rewriting of the passage in "Presence of an External Master of Knowledge" (*OP* 131), Stevens clarifies Ulysses' thought. He now says,

> "Here I feel the human loneliness
> And that, in space and solitude,
> Which knowledge is: the world and fate,
> The right within me and about me,
> Joined in a triumphant vigor,
> Like a direction on which I depend. . . ."

Just as Penelope in her loneliness senses "an inhuman meditation larger than her own," Ulysses senses what knowledge is "in space and solitude." He intuits that "the world and fate" are the knowledge of an external master, as the title tells us, and with this intuition he senses also that the knowledge "within [him]" is joined to that "about [him]." For Penelope the realization of the world as meditation provides the same comfort as Ulysses' return ("It was Ulysses and it was not"). For Ulysses, correspondingly, the realization of the world as knowledge is like the direction on which he depends for his return to Penelope.

The shorter poem is, however, more enigmatic on the relation between knowledge and being. Why are knowing and being one? Is it because Ulysses intuits that his being is a kind of knowledge, that reality itself, that which lies about him, corresponds on a larger scale to that which is within him? In the last stanza of his soliloquy in "Presence of an External Master of Knowledge" Ulysses says,

> "A longer, deeper breath sustains
> This eloquence of right, since knowing
> And being are one—the right to know
> Is equal to the right to be.
> The great Omnium descends on me,
> Like an absolute out of this eloquence."

This passage also raises a number of questions. Why does Ulysses in his isolation think of knowing and being as *rights*, which are normally conceived in social and political terms? What is the source of "This eloquence of right"? And what or who is the great Omnium, which descends like an absolute? The answer to the first question must surely be found in Stevens' concession to the language of the Columbia bicentennial, as Filreis has argued, and the word *right* stands out awkwardly in both poems as a sign of Stevens' inability to fuse twentieth-century ideology with Ulysses' more primitive epistemology.

The answers to the other two questions are found in the larger context of "The Sail of Ulysses," which projects two parallel lives and knowledges. In the fifth section of the poem, which corresponds to the passage above, Ulysses articulates his sense of the presence of the "longer, deeper breath" that sustains "The eloquence of right":

> "We come
> To knowledge when we come to life.
> Yet always there is another life,
> A life beyond this present knowing,
> A life lighter than this present splendor,
> Brighter, perfected and distant away,
> Not to be reached but to be known,
> Not an attainment of the will
> But something illogically received,

A divination, a letting down
From loftiness, misgivings dazzlingly
Resolved in dazzling discovery."

It is this second life or knowledge from which the "eloquence of right" is derived and from which the "great Omnium," that which contains all, descends like an "absolute."

The great Omnium, to put it more bluntly than Stevens wished to do in the poem, is what in the shorter poem he names the "External Master of Knowledge." In the longer version he is simply "Master of the world and of himself":

"His mind presents the world
And in his mind the world revolves.
The revolutions through day and night,
Through wild spaces of other suns and moons,
Round summer and angular winter and winds,
Are matched by other revolutions
In which the world goes round and round
In the crystal atmospheres of the mind. . . ."

What would the Phi Beta Kappa audience have made of such a fantasia if they had understood it? Perhaps here is the reason that Stevens "deliberately wrote an abstract poem," as Filreis reports he told Horace Taylor. Stevens found himself in the curious position of reading a poem so outlandish in its central conception that he did not wish to be fully understood. A poem that nods toward the bicentennial theme of "The Right to Knowledge" is in fact more interested in speculating on the "Presence of an External Master of Knowledge," as his shorter version indicates.

"The Sail of Ulysses" concludes by making explicit the link between Ulysses' prophetic utterances and his need or poverty, explaining why early in the poem he had said, "There is a human loneliness / . . . In which knowledge cannot be denied." The eighth canto begins, "What is the shape of the sibyl?" That is, what is the identity or source of Ulysses' transcendent knowledge, his awareness of "A life beyond this present knowing"? In answering this question, the poem dismisses the traditional conception of the sibyl as prophetess, "the englistered woman," the "gorgeous symbol seated / On the seat of halidom," the sibyl as holy seer. The sibyl or source of transcendent knowledge is instead the self—not, however, the normal self but the self in need, whose utter poverty becomes its greatest wealth:

> "It is the sibyl of the self,
> The self as sibyl, whose diamond,
> Whose chiefest embracing of all wealth
> Is poverty, whose jewel found
> At the exactest central of the earth
> Is need."

This passage—in fact, all of canto VIII of "The Sail of Ulysses"—serves as the most useful gloss on the union of poverty and transcendence that occurs throughout the poems of *The Rock*. It is this need, Ulysses argues, that creates the transcendent vision, the great Omnium, the External Master of Knowledge. In its need, the self as sibyl is "a blind thing fumbling for its form." Need provides the "right" to the kind of visionary knowledge Ulysses exemplifies; as a source, it is akin to what elsewhere in the poem is called "the credible thought / From which the incredible systems spring." The "Right to Knowledge," the bicentennial motto that provided the poem's ostensible theme, is in the end equated with the uses of need:

> "Need makes
> The right to use. Need names on its breath
> Categories of bleak necessity,
> Which, just to name, is to create
> A help, a right to help, a right
> To know what helps and to attain,
> By right of knowing, another plane."

This new plane, attained by "right of knowing" (a right accorded, in turn, by need), was presumably not the plane intended by the bicentennial committee when they suggested to Stevens his topic, and it is perhaps just as well that he refused to furnish them copies of the poem or to permit its publication in its original form. At the time the poem was written, as we know from the poems of *The Rock*, Stevens was more interested in his fiction of the world as meditation—the world *as* knowledge—than in the social or political implications of knowledge.

This interest offers an explanation of why the poem is so difficult, torn as it is between two irreconcilable themes, not disposed to make itself fully apparent. Its readers' disregard of one of these themes offers an explanation of why it has been, with a very few exceptions, so egregiously misread. Most readers have agreed with Frank Doggett's early assessment that the poem says the world "is known by each one only within his own mind and in terms of his personal realization," all of reality depending on "the instant of experience in one individual mind." The only readings of the poem I have located that merit consideration are those of Alan Filreis, Janet McCann, and Lucy Beckett, and as evidence of the poem's difficulty they run in different directions and reach very different conclusions. Filreis, as I have indicated, sets the poem solidly in its cultural context and works out convincingly the forces that dictate its language and its ostensible theme—though not, I think, its real theme. He disagrees with Beckett that it is "an occasional poem on an unpromising subject"; he argues that "issues of knowledge and freedom, mutually abridged rights, were just then so utterly promising as subjects for public oration that, if anything, Stevens was disappointed that he could not meet the matter's great potential *and* offer a poem to be deemed Stevensean." But this view disregards what Stevens told Babette Deutsch—that the subject, coupled with the public occasion, became "a force of intolerable generalities." In his reading, Filreis is also forced to disregard the great majority of the poem itself, which clearly does not grapple with the issues of mutually abridged rights. It is, on the whole, more

Stevensean than Filreis recognizes—not only in its covert theme but in its style, the late style to which Randall Jarrell so strongly objects, a manner "of thinking of particulars as primarily illustrations of general truths, or else as aesthetic, abstracted objects, simply there to be contemplated," a way of treating "things or lives so that they seem no more than generalizations of an unprecedentedly low order."[6]

In "The Sail of Ulysses" the reader is inundated in a succession of such generalizations. As Lucy Beckett notes, the poem "progresses not as a consecutive argument but as a proliferation of ideas set one against the other." She also notes what Filreis disregards, the poem's reach toward a form of transcendence, and she labels it "a religious meditation on knowledge as the precious connexion [sic] between the poor, lost, incomplete human being and that which can fulfil his need, find him, and make him whole." Of the passage in the poem's fifth canto where Ulysses speaks of "A life beyond this present knowing," she says, "A Christian would say that these lines are about grace, and that any other interpretation of them would be no more than a periphrasis for the theologian's single term." Beckett does not, however, discern the poem's central fiction of the world as the meditation or knowledge of an external master. She argues, in fact, that the poem gives evidence that "at last Stevens' thought has moved past the 'fictive covering' . . . to the nakedness of a timeless truth."[7]

Although she devotes only a paragraph to "The Sail of Ulysses" and "Presence of an External Master of Knowledge" in a chapter on Stevens' last poems, Janet McCann sees more clearly than other readers what lies at the center of both poems: "Ulysses, 'symbol of the seeker,' has found what he has long sought. At last he knows reality, and it knows him. He speaks, saying the words it intends for him to say." That is, quite correctly I think, she reads Ulysses' meditation on human loneliness, revised in the abridged version, as his acknowledgment that the external master of knowledge speaks through him. Note how the passage shifts in its significance when we apply that interpretation:

"Here I feel the human loneliness
And that, in space and solitude,
Which knowledge is: the world and fate,
The right within me and about me,
Joined in a triumphant vigor,
Like a direction on which I depend. . . ."

The poem, McCann concludes, depicts Ulysses meeting with "the other, unmediated and without form." Although its language is cryptic, it "implies a fated meeting with the outside imaginer. . . . Beyond the human imagination is the inhuman imagination, its mirror and creator."[8] What is odd is that so few readers have discerned this "fated meeting with the outside imaginer" in the poem despite Stevens' clues in the two shorter poems derived from it.

Published together in the *Times Literary Supplement* about three months after the Phi Beta Kappa reading, the shorter poems supply the intertext that makes "The Sail of Ulysses" intelligible—to the degree that it is. The title of one names the *presence* that had been so deeply buried as to be missed almost entirely by readers of the longer poem, as if Stevens were now stating explicitly what he had earlier hidden—"Presence of an External Master of Knowledge." Only the title of the other poem, "A Child Asleep in Its Own Life," is taken from "The Sail of Ulysses," but its argument is a gloss on its precursor. The line that serves as its title occurs in the final canto of the poem, when Ulysses is attempting to answer the question, "What is the shape of the sibyl?" What is the character of transcendent knowledge? The answer, as we have seen, is that the sibyl is the human self, although it has no shape. In its need, it is "a blind thing fumbling for its form," for "A dream too poor, too destitute / To be remembered." The "old shape" is "Worn and leaning to nothingness, / A woman looking down the road, / A child asleep in its own life." It is a stubbornly abstruse passage, but the figures of the woman and the child can be read as remnants of the memory that the self's new knowledge must accommodate, for Ulysses immediately says, "As these depend, so must they use." His conception of

"another plane" of knowledge both depends on and uses such frag-
ments of memory as "a child asleep in its own life."

The phrasing is odd, recalling the opening of "The Sail of
Ulysses," where Ulysses "read his own mind." The *own* here implies
the presence of another mind, just as the title "A Child Asleep in Its
Own Life" implies that there exists another, larger life that is not
asleep. And indeed that is what the poem says, in an unusually (for
Stevens) explicit manner. Except for the two last lines, its three stan-
zas do not present the enigmas of "The Sail of Ulysses" or "Presence
of an External Master of Knowledge."

> Among the old men that you know,
> There is one, unnamed, that broods
> On all the rest, in heavy thought.
>
> They are nothing, except in the universe
> Of that single mind. He regards them
> Outwardly and knows them inwardly,
>
> The sole emperor of what they are,
> Distant, yet close enough to wake
> The chords above your bed to-night.

Holly Stevens evidently thought the child was her son Peter and
asked one of her professors to interpret the poem, but he found it
"beyond" him.[9] Whether or not the child was Stevens' grandson,
the poem clearly has its source in an older man's memory of a
sleeping child contained in his waking mind, and it speculates on
various implications of sleeping and waking, outwardness and
inwardness, distance and closeness.

The occasion of watching a sleeping child is magnified to giant
proportions as a figure for reality itself, reality as the contents of a
mind. The "unnamed" old man is the "emperor" not of ice-cream,
but of "all the rest." (Although Stevens may have consciously
evoked the earlier poem, this emperor is not an object of sarcasm.)
The other old men do not exist "except in the universe / Of that sin-
gle mind" as he "broods" on them. They are regarded by him "out-

wardly" as objects of thought, but they are more importantly *known* "inwardly," since he is the "sole emperor" of "what they are," his own knowledge. When the persona says that this emperor is "Distant, yet close enough to wake / the chords above your bed to-night," he expresses the paradox of a cosmic meditation that is dis-tant in its largeness, containing a universe, yet close in its intimate knowledge of the contents of its mind, close enough to sing the child to sleep. It is tempting to suggest further that, despite the title, the "you" of the poem need not be a child; he is as easily the Stevens persona who assumes the role of the child in relation to the pater-nal mind in which he imagines himself contained. Milton Bates has noted how Stevens "found emotional as well as intellectual solace in playing child to this austere parent."[10] The title, then, may be sim-ply the trope on which the poem as a whole is based—reality as unconscious of itself as a part of a larger consciousness.

The poem's "universe / Of that single mind" bears some resem-blance to the earlier cosmic imagination of "The Auroras of Autumn" (*CP* 411), who also "meditates a whole . . . / As if he lived all lives," and Stevens returns to him indirectly in "Reality Is an Activity of the Most August Imagination" (*OP* 135). This poem of 1954 shares with "Presence of an External Master of Knowledge" the Stevensean title that states explicitly what the poem itself only hints at. (Throughout his career Stevens relied on titles to help solve the riddles posed by the poems.) If reality is indeed an activity of the most august (sublime, majestic, venerable) imagination, the only suggestion of this in the poem is its description of the aurora bore-alis, which in "The Auroras of Autumn" had been an emblem of such an imagination. But if the poem is, as it seems to me, a description of the aurora borealis, why have other accounts of it not made that identification? (Harold Bloom, for example, pointedly contrasts the "big light" of the poem to the aurora borealis of "The Auroras of Autumn.") It may be that the auroras have been unde-tected because they are associated in Stevens' readers' minds with autumn and this is a poem of summer. Further, what is here seen in a positive light was, in "The Auroras of Autumn," a source of fear: "The scholar of one candle sees / An Arctic effulgence flaring on the frame / Of everything he is. And he feels afraid." But the appearance of the auroras is not restricted to autumn; Harold Bloom himself reports seeing them in August,[11] which may be the month of this poem if Stevens is punning on the "August" of the title. Whatever the case, sightings occur in the northeastern United States during the summer months as well as the fall and winter.[12] And in regard to his speaker's more affirmative outlook in the later poem, Stevens' view of the cosmic imagination had clearly shifted between 1948, when "The Auroras of Autumn" was first published, and 1954. If the aurora borealis of autumn was commensurate with a destructive universal force, the auroras of summer represent "A vigor of glory," a sign of an "abstraction approaching form."

The poem depends for its effect on the difference in scale between this large abstraction and the small particular details of its opening lines—the names of the Connecticut towns,[13] the day of the week.

> Last Friday, in the big light of last Friday night,
> We drove home from Cornwall to Hartford, late.
>
> It was not a night blown at a glassworks in Vienna
> Or Venice, motionless, gathering time and dust.
>
> There was a crush of strength in a grinding going round,
> Under the front of the westward evening star,
>
> The vigor of glory, a glittering in the veins,
> As things emerged and moved and were dissolved,
>
> Either in distance, change or nothingness,
> The visible transformations of summer night,
>
> An argentine abstraction approaching form
> And suddenly denying itself away.
>
> There was an insolid billowing of the solid.
> Night's moonlight lake was neither water nor air.

In its initial context of a familiar drive from Cornwall to Hartford, the aurora borealis is only the "big light of last Friday night," but as the poem progresses it takes on the transcendence of its counterpart in "The Auroras of Autumn." Its effect is not that of an artificial and hence static concoction, something delicate made in Vienna or Venice. It is not the product of a human imagination; rather, it displays the energy and movement of something that has its own existence. And it is not merely alive but the agent of other lives, other things, coming into and out of existence. In its "visible transformations" it appears to display a will, as if it were pure principle verging on form and then consciously "denying itself" the form it approaches, transforming itself merely for the sake of transformation. It is this quality of the "big light" that more than anything else identifies it as the aurora borealis. Stevens' description consciously recalls the depiction of the same phenomenon—a cloud of color "lavishing . . . itself in change" because "it likes magnificence"—in the sixth and seventh cantos of "The Auroras of Autumn." The obvious difference is that the auroras' transformations now provide an affirmative knowledge that intensifies and heightens the evening as an "activity" of an external imagination.

In "Solitaire under the Oaks" (*OP* 137) and "A Clear Day and No Memories" (*OP* 138), the opposite phenomenon is observed. That is, the *absence* of activity leads to the awareness of the world as knowledge, sense, or abstraction. In the first poem, the "oblivion" of a game of solitaire under the oak trees releases the speaker from consciousness and suggests what it would be like to "escape / To principium, to meditation," as if "One exist[ed] among pure principles." In the second, as the title suggests, the absence of memories is identified with a condition of weather, a clear day, although the poem at first appears to say the opposite:

> No soldiers in the scenery,
> No thoughts of people now dead,
> As they were fifty years ago:
> Young and living in a live air,
> Young and walking in the sunshine,

> Bending in blue dresses to touch something—
> Today the mind is not part of the weather.

The stanza engages in what P. Michael Campbell and John Dolan
have labeled "praeteritic antithesis," a rhetorical move in which the
rejected terms become dominant. The lines are composed of mem-
ories that the speaker denies, as if, in accordance with Freud's the-
ory of negation, he could bring them to consciousness in such con-
crete terms—women in blue dresses bending down to touch
something—only by prefacing them with "No." In his essay "Nega-
tion," Freud says that when certain associations are voluntarily
offered in a negative form, we are justified in "disregarding the
negation and picking out the subject-matter alone of the associa-
tion."[14] According to Freud's principle, we are justified in our infer-
ence that Stevens' speaker is in reality saying that it is a day of mem-
ories of the dead as they were fifty years ago. The same is true of the
final line. Why does he say that the mind is *not* part of the weather?
Why is the weather suddenly interjected into a discussion of mem-
ories? And are we justified in disregarding the "not" and concen-
trating on the association? What does a mind supposedly (but not
actually) free from memories have to do with the weather?

It is in fact the state of the weather on this particular day that
suggests a state of mind. "Today the mind is not part of the
weather," we learn in the second stanza, because the weather gives
the appearance of a clear mind with no knowledge of its contents,
in the same manner that the speaker claims to have no memories.

> Today the air is clear of everything.
> It has no knowledge except of nothingness
> And it flows over us without meanings,
> As if none of us had ever been here before
> And are not now: in this shallow spectacle,
> This invisible activity, this sense.

"In the poem's final word," George Lensing writes, Stevens "con-
cedes his own presence as a 'sense,' one perceiving, one making

meanings, one who sees and breathes and knows the air of the 'clear day.'" This would be a reasonable way to read the stanza if "A Clear Day and No Memories" were a much earlier poem. Daniel Schwarz likewise says of the poem that it is "the individual minds of all of us in quest of meaning that are the speaker's concerns."[15] The individual quest for meaning, it is true, was Stevens' speakers' concerns through much of his canon, but in 1955 that concern has been displaced. In its context in the passage, it is clearly not the speaker's own sense to which he refers. The "sense" in question is in apposition to "this shallow spectacle, / This invisible activity," which in turn clearly refer to the weather, the air that is "clear of everything." The stanza as a whole is a description of a clear day's apparent lack of knowledge, which parallels the speaker's apparent lack of memory: "*It* has no knowledge except of nothingness." The quality of the day's weather is such that it seems as if the air flows "without meanings" over those who reside in it—"without meanings," that is, for the day's clear air, which is now conceived as a kind of knowledge or sense. Just as the speaker claims that those who were alive fifty years ago do not occupy his memory on this day, his claim for the day is that those who dwell in it do not occupy its memory: "As if none of us had ever been here before," and, what is more, "are not now." But here is another instance of Campbell's and Dolan's praeteritic antithesis. In order to suggest the day's apparent lack of activity, the speaker must attribute to it an "invisible activity"; in order to suggest its lack of knowledge, he must attribute to it a kind of knowledge, "this sense." Stevens had used a similar strategy earlier in *The Rock,* where in "Vacancy in the Park" a sense of presence is conveyed by absence.

"A Clear Day and No Memories" and "Solitaire under the Oaks" were published with "Local Objects" (*OP* 137) and "Artificial Populations" (*OP* 138) in the *Sewanee Review* in January 1955, the last poems Stevens published. "Local Objects" goes off in a slightly different direction; in a "world without a foyer," an entry into another world, it says, "local objects become / More precious." "Artificial Populations" is, however, very much in the mode of "A Clear Day and No Memories" and casts some light on it. It considers the same parallel between the mind and the weather, which now becomes a "centre," one of Stevens' code words, along with "central" (as in "central man") for an ideal or transcendent presence:

> The centre that he sought was a state of mind,
> Nothing more, like weather after it has cleared—
> Well, more than that, like weather when it has cleared
> And the two poles continue to maintain it
>
> And the Orient and the Occident embrace
> To form the weather's appropriate people,
> The rosy men and the women of the rose,
> Astute in being what they are made to be.

At first reading the speaker appears to be saying that he wishes to achieve a state of mind that is like weather after it has cleared, but as the poem progresses it appears more likely that the "centre" he looks for is an external state of mind. It also seems likely, although the poem is hesitant to say it outright, that the "artificial populations" of the title, men and women "Astute in being what they are made to be," are creations—from one point of view, artifacts—of this external mind or sense, which Stevens describes less hesitantly in "A Clear Day and No Memories," the poem that follows "Artificial Populations" in their ordering in the *Sewanee Review.*

"Artificial Populations" is a much more difficult poem than "A Clear Day"—one could even accuse it of incoherence at certain key points—but it seems to repeat one of the motifs of "The Rock" (*CP* 525), the notion that reality and its inhabitants are created as an "illusion" by an external consciousness to satisfy "its own happiness," as Stevens puts it in the earlier poem, or to cure some deficiency. In "The Rock" the reality created by the "fantastic consciousness" is "like a blindness cleaned, / Exclaiming bright sight, as it was satisfied, / In a birth of sight." In "Artificial Populations" the "weather's appropriate people" are created to heal a sickness, to satisfy a deep need, in the way that angels were created to satisfy the need for heaven:

This artificial population is like
A healing-point in the sickness of the mind:
Like angels resting on a rustic steeple
Or a confect of leafy faces in a tree—

A health—and the faces in a summer night.

The last line recalls an earlier fantastic consciousness, that of "Credences of Summer" (*CP* 372), in which "The personae of summer play the characters / Of an inhuman author" on a summer night, just as the "rosy" men and women of "Artificial Populations" recall the "roseate characters" of the earlier poem. "Credences of Summer" marked the first extended appearance of Stevens' external consciousness, and "Artificial Populations" and "A Clear Day and No Memories," published just months before his death, mark the last.

"Credences of Summer" is one of four earlier poems alluded to in the most autobiographical of the late poems, "As You Leave the Room" (*OP* 117). It is probable (though not certain) that it was written at the same time as the other uncollected poems, given its performance of leave-taking, the poet's survey of an entire career from the perspective afforded by the finale. It is this perspective and the poet's allusion to earlier identifiable poems that have led to its quite appropriate comparison to Yeats' "The Circus Animals' Desertion." But there is one crucial difference between the two. Yeats' review poem begins with his questioning of his present powers of imagination; although the poem itself gives the lie to it, his claim is that his imagination has deserted him in old age and he must be satisfied to rehearse old themes. Stevens' review poem, to the contrary, questions the foundation of his *earlier* poetry—its approach to reality—on the basis of his present grasp of reality, which he clearly privileges.

"As You Leave the Room" is a reworking of an unpublished poem of 1947 titled "First Warmth." Stevens had inscribed "First Warmth" on the title page of the copy of *Transport to Summer* belonging to Herbert Weinstock, his editor at Knopf,[16] and most accounts of the poem have centered on the differences between the two versions, deducing Stevens' intentions in "As You Leave the Room" from the changes he made in the earlier, shorter version. Although the differences have been overstated, they are instructive. Here is "First Warmth" (*OP* 117):

> I wonder, have I lived a skeleton's life,
> As a questioner about reality,
>
> A countryman of all the bones in the world?
> Now, here, the warmth I had forgotten becomes
>
> Part of the major reality, part of
> An appreciation of a reality;
>
> And thus an elevation, as if I lived
> With something I could touch, touch every way.

The poem is a variation of a theme from very early Stevens; the first warmth of spring reminds the Stevens-like speaker (both versions are unguardedly personal) of a reality to which he had been insensible, dead, "A countryman of all the bones in the world." "The Sun This March" (*CP* 133) from *Ideas of Order* states its earlier variant not in terms of warmth but of brightness: "The exceeding brightness of this early sun / Makes me conceive how dark I have become." "First Warmth" goes beyond this seasonal motif, however, to suggest the possibility of an entire lifetime of insensibility to the "major reality" of which the Stevens persona, "Now, here," is a part.

When Stevens rewrote the poem, possibly in 1955, he encased the original lines in a poem exactly twice as long, with six new lines preceding the earlier version and two lines following it. The new title appropriately identifies it as a poem of the end: rooms, foyers, and houses occur frequently in the late poems as emblems of larger worlds or states of being, as in "The Irish Cliffs of Moher" (*CP* 501) from *The Rock*, where the speaker asks, "Who is my father in this world, in this house, / At the spirit's base?"[17] By its title alone, "As

You Leave the Room" announces itself as a finale, a conclusion "Here at life's end" (as Yeats puts it in one of his last poems) in a manner that "First Warmth" does not. Here is the revision, whose departures from the earlier version are readily apparent even though their significance has not been quite so obvious:

> *You speak. You say:* Today's character is not
> A skeleton out of its cabinet. Nor am I.
>
> That poem about the pineapple, the one
> About the mind as never satisfied,
>
> The one about the credible hero, the one
> About summer, are not what skeletons think about.
>
> I wonder, have I lived a skeleton's life,
> As a disbeliever in reality,
>
> A countryman of all the bones in the world?
> Now, here, the snow I had forgotten becomes
>
> Part of a major reality, part of
> An appreciation of a reality
>
> And thus an elevation, as if I left
> With something I could touch, touch every way.
>
> And yet nothing has been changed except what is
> Unreal, as if nothing had been changed at all.

In adapting his earlier lines Stevens has made four changes: "a questioner about reality" has been intensified to "a disbeliever in reality"; "warmth" has been inverted to "snow"; "*the* major reality" is now only "*a* major reality"; and, in keeping with the new title, "lived" is now a more fateful "left."

In an extended discussion of the two versions, John Dolan

argues that the revision—and he means both these changes and the additional lines—"reverses the entire argument of 'First Warmth.' The successive versions constitute an antinomy, a purposeful juxtaposition of conflicting or contradictory positions." He bases this judgment on his assumption that "As You Leave the Room" answers the doubt of the earlier poem, asserting that "the poet is no kin to 'skeletons.'" Likewise, in a recent analysis of the two versions, Lee Jenkins, who appears to believe that the first version is superior to the second, which is "equivocal," argues that "each revision of 'First Warmth' is also a retreat from the candour of 'First Warmth.'"[18] The conclusions of both readers are, I believe, limited by their assumptions about the import of Stevens' revisions. "As You Leave the Room" is not, as I think can be demonstrated, a reversal of the position of "First Warmth"; it constitutes not a retreat from or a softening of that position, but a more severe judgment of the poet's earlier self. It is true that version two advances a more complicated point of view in splitting the poet into a "you" and "I," self and soul (another affinity with the late Yeats), but both poems ask the same question and arrive at the same conclusion. The revisions have more to do with tailoring the poem to its new status as a farewell to a life of poetry than with softening it or reversing its position.

The shift from "questioner about reality" to "disbeliever in reality" indicates the harshness of the older poet's judgment of his younger self. It is a shift from mere philosophical scepticism to religious failure of belief, an error of greater severity to the present believer in reality, although he is now willing to concede, more modestly, that it is "*a* major reality," an "appreciation of *a* reality," and not, definitively and naively, *the* reality. The other two changes merely reflect the shift in the title, which in turn announces the poem's new position in the poet's canon. Stevens removes "warmth" from version two because the title and the metaphor it implied—the coming of spring—were inappropriate to a poem of approaching death; the "snow" here is in keeping with the general barrenness and poverty of the winter landscape of the poems of *The Rock* and after. The need to reposition the poem is also responsible for the change from "lived" to "left" in "as if I lived / With something I could touch, touch every way." "First Warmth" is a poem about spring as a reminder to the poet of something he had forgotten, perhaps temporarily. "As You Leave the Room" is a poem about the poet's parting words as he judges the poems of a career, and in this context "left" is a necessary revision, and the only word in the poem that picks up the implications of the title. Dolan and Jenkins, it seems to me, exaggerate the importance of these revisions, which have a great deal to do simply with the poet's craft—an alteration of the poem's underlying metaphor.

Yet even with these changes, and the harsher wording of version two, the poems still ask the same question: "I wonder, have I lived a skeleton's life . . . ?" There are any number of reasons why one may ask such a question and many versions of it. "Do any human beings ever realize life while they live it?" This version, from Wilder's *Our Town*, which I cited in the discussion of "To an Old Philosopher in Rome," is not irrelevant here, especially since the answer is "The saints and poets, maybe—they do some."[19] I argued there that Stevens places George Santayana as the secular saint in the company of those who have realized life—"realized" is the final word of the poem—although this realization takes place only at the very end, only as he is leaving it. In "As You Leave the Room" Stevens makes the same claim for himself.

The poet wonders if he has lived a skeleton's life because he now sees that he has been a disbeliever in reality. And he recognizes his earlier disbelief precisely because of his present belief. It is significant that the turn in both versions begins "Now, here. . . ." It is from the perspective of his accord with reality as he leaves the room—now, here—that he questions a lifetime of scepticism and denial: "Now, here, the snow I had forgotten becomes / Part of a major reality / An appreciation of a reality. . . ." "To an Old Philosopher in Rome" (*CP* 508) concludes of Santayana as he leaves the room: "He stops upon this threshold, / As if the design of all his words take form / And frame from thinking and is realized." Stevens' reality similarly takes form, "as if I left / With something I could touch, touch every way." "As You Leave the Room" rewrites "To an Old Philosopher" in yet one further way. One phenomenon of Santayana's threshold experience is that the ordinary objects of his convent room take on new significance as they are "realized"— made real—yet curiously remain unchanged: "It is a kind of total grandeur at the end, / With every visible thing enlarged and yet / No more than a bed, a chair and moving nuns." It is with a close variant of this phenomenon that "As You Leave the Room" concludes in a couplet that has eluded its readers: "And yet nothing has been changed except what is / Unreal, as if nothing had been changed at all." George Lensing writes of this passage that it "reaffirms the presence of nothingness" and that "the unreal projections of [Stevens'] own subjectivity . . . have, in fact, rescued him from his malaise and renewed him." John Dolan says that "what is 'Unreal' has been affirmed."[20] Neither reading could be further from what the passage in fact says, that the world that was "unreal" to the disbeliever in reality, Stevens' earlier self, has been changed to the real, although, like the objects of Santayana's convent room, it gives no outward appearance of this change. To put it in the poem's terms, "And yet nothing has been changed except what is / Unreal [to what is real], as if nothing had been changed at all."

Readers have been thrown off course by the poem's structure and point of view. Because it has always been read alongside "First Warmth," its opening six lines have been something of a puzzle. They appear to refute the notion that the poet has "lived a skeleton's life" even before it has been introduced into the poem. That is, the ordering of the poem seems at first odd because the answer to the charge precedes the charge. The opening lines (apparently) refute the charge by alluding to four poems that are "not what skeletons think about": "Someone Puts a Pineapple Together," "The Well Dressed Man with a Beard," "Examination of the Hero in a Time of War," and "Credences of Summer." Three of these might fairly be characterized as poems in quest of the real and the fourth, "Someone Puts a Pineapple Together," although it might seem an anomaly because it is a poem about artifice, merits inclusion because it appears as a demonstration in a lecture, "Three Academic Pieces," which argues that "reality is the central reference for poetry" (*NA*

71). But why should these six lines not follow the passage revised from "First Warmth" that begins, "I wonder, have I lived a skeleton's life"? In that case the sequence of the poem would have been: Have I lived a skeleton's life? No. I have written poems that are not what skeletons think about.

But that is not quite what the poem says. It is an internal debate—the "I wonder" even of the first version points in this direction—in which the poet is able to separate himself into a "you" who speaks for his younger self, the author of the four poems cited, and a present "I." This explains its curious opening, which goes to some lengths to underscore the point that the first six lines are not spoken by the "I" of the remainder of the poem: "*You speak. You say:* Today's character is not / A skeleton out of its cabinet." "I wonder," the "I" says in response. In spite of what you say, "have I lived a skeleton's life?" The remainder of the poem suggests that it is the second position, that of the "I," that it adopts. He *has* lived a skeleton's life, but its unreality has become "a major reality" as he leaves it. And perhaps, as in the case of Santayana and many of the other personae of *The Rock,* his leaving it is a necessary condition of its becoming real.

If "As You Leave the Room" is about leaving, then "Of Mere Being" (*OP* 141) may be thought of as a poem about *after* leaving or *beyond* leaving. Yeats' frightful image of life without him (in "The Apparitions") was an empty coat on a coat hanger; Stevens' image of what is "Beyond the last thought" (which may or may not be eschatological) is a very Yeatsian golden bird in a palm tree. The poem has attracted more commentary than any other of the uncollected poems in part because it is legendarily Stevens' last poem—Holly Stevens placed it last in her chronologically-arranged collection and took its first line as her title—and in part because it has been thought to say something profound (Harold Bloom calls it "mysterious and definitive").[21] Alone of the poems of Stevens' last two years, it has been rigorously read and debated, its cruxes and difficulties laid out for scrutiny. I will resist adding yet another full-scale reading to a long and distinguished list that includes Bloom's early intertextual analysis, still one of the most convincing, and a recent reading by Jennifer Bates that examines in great detail the issues the poem has generated. What engages me in the poem is not perhaps its most significant aspect. I am interested in Stevens' (necessarily failed) attempt to construct an image of a state of being that exists apart from the human mind and human reason. That is, I want to read "Of Mere Being" as a final fiction that mirrors the larger fiction of the late poetry, in which Stevens' cosmic imagination is the central component of a project to imagine a reality paradoxically independent of the imagination.

In poems like "Final Soliloquy of the Interior Paramour" and "Not Ideas about the Thing but the Thing Itself" Stevens is successful in discovering a way to posit a reality outside the human mind. In "Final Soliloquy" this external reality is, quite convincingly, the felt presence of "an order, a whole, / A knowledge, that which arranged the rendezvous / Within *its* vital boundary, in the mind" (*CP* 524; my italics). In "Not Ideas about the Thing" the earliest sound of spring, a bird's cry, is forced outside the mind. It is not part of "the vast ventriloquism / Of sleep's faced papier-mâché," ideas about the thing. The bird's cry is "part of the colossal sun" and, finally, "like / A new knowledge of reality" (*CP* 534), the thing itself, spring as a part of an external knowledge. A variation of this project to imagine an independent reality can be seen in late poems like "A Clear Day and No Memories," discussed earlier, in which an external reality is essentially indifferent to the human. Here the air "has no knowledge except of nothingness / And it flows over us without meanings." Similarly, in "The Region November" (*OP* 140), a poem of Stevens' last year, the sound of swaying trees is "On the level of that which is not yet knowledge: / A revelation not yet intended." In "The Course of a Particular" (*OP* 123), which was omitted from *The Rock* by mistake (see *Letters* 881), the persona "feels the life of that which gives life as it is" in "the cry of leaves that do not transcend themselves." It is "not a cry of divine attention" but a cry, finally, that "concerns no one at all."

It is in the context of poems such as these that "Of Mere Being" yields its most overt or manifest meaning. The *mere* being of its title is both *no more than* being in current usage and *pure* or *absolute* being in the older sense of the word, being uncontaminated by the mind's perspective or the scrutiny of the reason. The poem's image of mere being is "at the end of the mind, / Beyond the last thought." Questions immediately arise. Is mere being "Beyond the last thought" because it is ineffable, beyond thought in that it cannot be captured by thought or expressed in words? Is it beyond the last thought because it is beyond life, beyond the last thought that precedes death? Or, finally, is it beyond thought in that it is not a creation of the mind, not a construction of thought or reason? Different answers to the first two questions have divided the commentary on the poem (the third question has not often been asked), but one could argue without really hedging that there is a point at which these distinctions cease to matter. The poem attempts to posit a conception of being that is sundered absolutely from the human mind and thus necessarily survives "the end of the mind" in death. It would appear, in fact, that Stevens' ambiguity in "at the end of the mind" and "Beyond the last thought" functions precisely to incorporate both the epistemological and eschatological implications of his conception of being. (Jennifer Bates asks whether the epistemological and eschatological meanings are even different for Stevens.)[22]

None of the possible interpretations of "Beyond the last thought," however, escape the contradiction that is central to the poem. If pure being is beyond the last thought in any of the three senses above, then how is it possible to depict it, to provide an image for it, as the poem attempts to do? This is a version of the difficulty Stevens confronts in his fiction of the cosmic imagination. His attempt to theorize a reality that is not simply a projection of the imagination requires a supreme act of imagination. It is a quandary that he recognizes in the late poems. "Yet the absence of the imagination had / Itself to be imagined," he admits in "The Plain Sense of Things" (*CP* 502); although the lines mean something more than they appear to, they mean that also. Some of the difficulties of the later poetry—its evasions, abstractions, and resistance to paraphrase—may be traced to Stevens' attempts to conceal his dilemma, and "Of Mere Being" unmasks it perhaps more clearly than any other of the last poems.

The dilemma of the poem is that mere being must be beyond the mind or thought (since it is no "mere" mental conception) and, at the same time, capable of being fully realized. Otherwise the Stevens persona could not say, after depicting an image of it, "You know then that it is not the reason / That makes us happy or unhappy." That is, once one recognizes the existence of pure being, a reality independent of the mind or reason, one understands how little the reason has to do with the pleasures and sorrows of our lives. Stevens' way out of this dilemma is to depict mere being in an image that is fully realized yet oddly beyond explication, "without human meaning":

> The palm at the end of the mind,
> Beyond the last thought, rises
> In the bronze decor,
>
> A gold-feathered bird
> Sings in the palm, without human meaning,
> Without human feeling, a foreign song.
>
> You know then that it is not the reason
> That makes us happy or unhappy.
> The bird sings. Its feathers shine.
>
> The palm stands on the edge of space.
> The wind moves slowly in the branches.
> The bird's fire-fangled feathers dangle down.

The bird and palm share with the weather of "A Clear Day and No Memories," the trees and leaves of "The Region November" and "The Course of a Particular," the absence of human meaning, and because of the nature of its images "Of Mere Being" is more successful than the other poems in indicating this absence.

In "'A mythology reflects its region . . .'" (*OP* 141), a poem written about the same time as "Of Mere Being," Stevens says, "The image must be of the nature of its creator." The mythologist's images are "the substance of his region, / Wood of his forests and stone out of his fields / Or from under his mountains." Curiously, however, Stevens' mythology of being selects images that are foreign to his region. Yet the palm and its gold-feathered bird are selected precisely because they are foreign, like the bird's song, without human feeling or meaning. Readers have heard Yeats' "Sailing to Byzantium" in the poem, and the presence of Yeats' golden bird is undeniable. Yeats' artificial bird is set against the natural birds of the poem's opening; it is "out of nature." Stevens' exotic palm and golden bird in their static "bronze decor" are equally "out of nature," although for a slightly different reason. Yeats' poem privileges art over life; Stevens' presumed last poem privileges an ineffable and non-human reality over the mind and the reason. That is why the poem seems remote from human concerns and why its central image is ultimately inexplicable.[23]

The poem as a whole is not, however, unreadable, and it has been accorded a more sympathetic reception than any other of the uncollected poems. At the conclusion of his discussion of Stevens in *The Poems of Our Climate,* Bloom calls it "Stevens' ultimate vision," and Jennifer Bates labels it "a poem of supreme fiction" that "uncovers . . . a final relationship to being." Although its enigmatic quality is always conceded, the reader, for once in the late poems, "more or less feels what this poem means," as Randall Jarrell said about another of Stevens' difficult poems.[24] One of the ironies of its appreciative reception is that after so many efforts to disclose an external reality beyond the constructs of the mind, the pervasive fiction of the late poems that his readers have been slow to acknowledge, Stevens seems to have come closest to imparting it to them in what may have been his final attempt, in the last of the last poems.

NOTES

NOTES TO PREFACE

1. Harold Bloom, *Wallace Stevens: The Poems of Our Climate* (Ithaca, 1977), 338.
2. Michael Riffaterre, *Semiotics of Poetry* (Bloomington, 1978), 164–65.
3. Charles Berger, *Forms of Farewell: The Late Poetry of Wallace Stevens* (Madison, 1985), xi.

NOTES TO CHAPTER 1

1. William York Tindall, *Wallace Stevens* (Minneapolis, 1961), 32; Joseph Riddel, *The Clairvoyant Eye: The Poetry and Poetics of Wallace Stevens* (Baton Rouge, 1965), 275; Robert Rehder, *The Poetry of Wallace Stevens* (London, 1988), 219; Daniel R. Schwarz, *Narrative and Representation in the Poetry of Wallace Stevens* (New York, 1993), 149; Rajeev S. Patke, *The Long Poems of Wallace Stevens: An Interpretative Study* (Cambridge, 1985), 117. I must admit to having once held the same view. See *Wallace Stevens and Poetic Theory* (Chapel Hill, 1987), 55.
2. David R. Jarraway, *Wallace Stevens and the Question of Belief: Metaphysician in the Dark* (Baton Rouge, 1993), 141, 142, 174.
3. Janet McCann, *Wallace Stevens Revisited: "The Celestial Possible"* (New York, 1995), 101, 120, 137.
4. Joseph Carroll, *Wallace Stevens' Supreme Fiction: A New Romanticism* (Baton Rouge, 1987), 9, 303, 309, 313.
5. Ibid., 260.
6. Bloom, *Poems of Our Climate*, 251–52; Riddel, *Clairvoyant Eye*, 221; Helen Vendler, *On Extended Wings: Wallace Stevens' Longer Poems* (Cambridge, Mass., 1969), 243, 245.
7. Jarraway, *Wallace Stevens and the Question of Belief*, 232.
8. Vendler, *On Extended Wings*, 231.
9. This fiction should not be confused with one of the master tropes of the early poetry, which Dorothy Emerson calls "the sky as mind," the use of natural objects

as "symbolic replications of the mind in action." For a discussion of this figure see Emerson's "Wallace Stevens' Sky That Thinks," *Wallace Stevens Journal* 9 (1985): 71–84.

10. Carroll, *Wallace Stevens' Supreme Fiction,* 309.

11. Ibid., 309–10.

12. In a recent discussion of the poem, David Humphries also notes that it echoes the enthroned imagination passage in "The Auroras of Autumn." He does not, however, recognize the presence of this inhuman imagination in "The Plain Sense of Things." His argument is that the poem exhibits a "new kind of meditation" on Stevens' part that leads, in turn, to "a new sense of perception and a new sense of identity, one more in harmony with our modern understanding of nature." See his "A New Kind of Meditation: Wallace Stevens' 'The Plain Sense of Things,'" *Wallace Stevens Journal* 23 (1999): 38, 47.

13. Humphries argues, to the contrary, that the "fantastic" imagination is the poet's former imagination: "the old, 'fantastic' imagination has dissolved, and a new imagination and a new reality are in the process of being conceived." Ibid., 44.

14. Anthony Whiting, *The Never-Resting Mind: Wallace Stevens' Romantic Irony* (Ann Arbor, 1996), 168.

15. In "The Auroras of Autumn" the cosmic imagination is not free to act "by chance" but must follow some necessary law that is not clearly specified. In the parodic "Looking across the Fields and Watching the Birds Fly," the "pensive nature" is described as "a mechanical / And slightly detestable *operandum.*" Stevens also associates necessity with the "angel of reality" of "Angel Surrounded by Paysans" (*CP* 496), a variant of the godlike imagination of the later poems.

16. Barbara Johnson, "*Les Fleurs du mal armé:* Some Reflections on Intertextuality," in *Lyric Poetry: Beyond the New Criticism,* ed. Chaviva Hosek and Patricia Parker (Ithaca, 1985), 265.

17. In the fifth chapter I attempt to show how Miller's weak misreading of "The Rock" can be traced in part to his inability to read the poem's intertext of reality as the invention of a "fantastic consciousness."

NOTES TO CHAPTER 2

1. See also Wallace Stevens, *The Palm at the End of the Mind: Selected Poems and a Play,* ed. Holly Stevens (New York, 1972), xv.

2. Michael Hobbs assumes that the *your*s are addressed to Stevens' "imagined reader," and that the poem is a "dialogic exchange" in which the "authorial mantle" is surrendered to the reader. See his "Stevens' Gunman Lover: Readers in *The Rock,*" *Wallace Stevens Journal* 18 (1994): 159. That interpretation, however, ignores the fact that every quality preceded by *your* stands in apposition to the two worlds asleep and, in turn, to the "Old Man" of the title.

3. Eleanor Cook, *Poetry, Word-Play, and Word-War in Wallace Stevens* (Princeton, 1988), 297.

4. Robert Pogue Harrison, "'Not Ideas about the Thing but the Thing Itself,'" *New Literary History* 30 (1999): 667.

5. Edward Kessler, *Images of Wallace Stevens* (New Brunswick, 1972), 85; Frank Doggett, *Stevens' Poetry of Thought* (Baltimore, 1966), 179; Berger, *Forms of Farewell*, 168–70; Thomas Lombardi, *Wallace Stevens and the Pennsylvania Keystone: The Influence of Origins on His Life and Poetry* (Selinsgrove, 1996), 217.

6. Lombardi, *Wallace Stevens and the Pennsylvania Keystone,* 213; William Burney, *Wallace Stevens* (New York, 1968), 165.

7. The book is now in the Wallace Stevens Collection of the Huntington Library. See Robert Moynihan, "Checklist: Second Purchase, Wallace Stevens Collection, Huntington Library," *Wallace Stevens Journal* 20 (1996): 97.

8. One of the senses of the plural form of *Lebensweisheit* is aphorisms or *aperçus.*

9. Richard P. Adams, "Wallace Stevens and Schopenhauer's *The World as Will and Idea,*" *Tulane Studies in English* 20 (1972): 135–36. Adams finds Schopenhauer's presence in a number of Stevens' poems, including "The Snow Man," "Tea at the Palaz of Hoon," "The Man with the Blue Guitar," "Notes toward a Supreme Fiction," and "An Ordinary Evening in New Haven."

10. William V. Davis, "'This Refuge That the End Creates': Stevens' 'Not Ideas about the Thing but the Thing Itself,'" *Wallace Stevens Journal* 11 (1987): 104.

11. Arthur Kenyon Rogers, *A Student's History of Philosophy,* 3rd ed. (New York, 1932), 427, 434.

12. Helen Regueiro, *The Limits of Imagination: Wordsworth, Yeats, and Stevens* (Ithaca, 1976), 204.

13. Ibid.

NOTES TO CHAPTER 3

1. Lucy Beckett, *Wallace Stevens* (London, 1974), 190.

2. Whiting, *Never-Resting Mind,* 166; Richard Blessing, *Wallace Stevens' "Whole Harmonium"* (Syracuse, 1970), 167; Kessler, *Images of Wallace Stevens,* 86; Ronald Sukenick, *Wallace Stevens: Musing the Obscure* (New York, 1967), 192; Denis Donoghue, *Connoisseurs of Chaos: Ideas of Order in Modern American Poetry,* 2nd ed. (New York, 1984), 15.

3. McCann, *Wallace Stevens Revisited,* 131.

4. Bloom, *Poems of Our Climate,* 359.

5. Ibid.; Barbara Fisher, *Wallace Stevens: The Intensest Rendezvous* (Charlottesville, 1990), 85; Adalaide Kirby Morris, *Wallace Stevens: Imagination and Faith* (Princeton, 1974), 88; Carroll, *Wallace Stevens' Supreme Fiction,* 310; Jacqueline

Vaught Brogan, "'Sisters of the Minotaur': Sexism and Stevens," in *Wallace Stevens and the Feminine,* ed. Melita Schaum (Tuscaloosa, 1993), 16; Mary Arensberg, "'A Curable Separation': Stevens and the Mythology of Gender," in *Wallace Stevens and the Feminine,* 27, 40.

6. Barbara Fisher, "A Woman with the Hair of a Pythoness," in *Wallace Stevens and the Feminine,* 48.

7. Thomas C. Grey, *The Wallace Stevens Case: Law and the Practice of Poetry* (Cambridge, Mass., 1991), 49; Carroll, *Wallace Stevens' Supreme Fiction,* 310; Arensberg, "'Curable Separation,'" 40.

8. I am not the only reader who has noted that the poem may posit some external order. Charles Berger opens this possibility in a series of questions: "What is the referent in 'that which arranged the rendezvous, / Within its vital boundary, in the mind'? . . . [M]ight not the force which arranged the rendezvous be a force for the *other* side? Similarly, does 'an order, a whole, a knowledge' refer to the 'collect' Stevens has now become, or does it point to something beyond thim?" *Forms of Farewell,* 172. Berger, however, reads "Final Soliloquy" as a poem about "crossing over" into death, so he associates the external force in question with the "*other* side," death.

9. Ibid.; Bloom, *Poems of Our Climate,* 359; Arensberg, "'Curable Separation,'" 40.

10. The two poems were published in the *Hudson Review* in a group of eight poems that included "To an Old Philosopher in Rome," which also profits from being read together with "Final Soliloquy of the Interior Paramour."

11. George Lensing, *Wallace Stevens: A Poet's Growth* (Baton Rouge, 1986), 201, 221.

12. Ibid., 222.

13. Doggett, *Stevens' Poetry of Thought,* 172.

14. Ulysses would have approached from the east had he returned directly from Troy. He returns, however, from the island of the Phaeacians, which many commentators identify as modern Corfu, northwest of Ithaca.

15. Randall Jarrell, "Randall Jarrell Discovers 'a Great Poem of a New Kind,'" in *Wallace Stevens: The Critical Heritage,* ed. Charles Doyle (London, 1985), 423; Bloom, *Poems of Our Climate,* 363; Beckett, *Wallace Stevens,* 199; George Lensing, *Wallace Stevens and the Seasons* (Baton Rouge, 2001), 192; Burney, *Wallace Stevens,* 169; Arensberg, "'Curable Separation,'" 42; Blessing, *Wallace Stevens' "Whole Harmonium,"* 56; Mark Halliday, *Stevens and the Interpersonal* (Princeton, 1991), 183; Loren Rusk, "Penelope's Creative Desiring: 'The World as Meditation,'" *Wallace Stevens Journal* 9 (1985): 21, 23, 22.

16. Bloom, *Poems of Our Climate,* 363, 364; Arensberg, "'Curable Separation,'" 42; Rusk, "Penelope's Creative Desiring," 16; Halliday, *Stevens and the Interpersonal,* 68; Frank Lentricchia, *Modernist Quartet* (Cambridge, 1994), 173; Lensing, *Wallace Stevens and the Seasons,* 197–98.

17. Lentricchia, *Modernist Quartet,* 175, 176; Fisher, *Intensest Rendezvous,* 15; Lensing, *Wallace Stevens and the Seasons,* 195.

18. Rusk, "Penelope's Creative Desiring," 23; Doggett, *Stevens' Poetry of Thought,* 172; C. Roland Wagner, "Wallace Stevens: The Concealed Self," in *Wallace Stevens and the Feminine,* 135; Fisher, *Intensest Rendezvous,* 18.

19. Schopenhauer is associated not with Homburg but with Hamburg, where the family moved in 1793 when he was five years old. His father, a successful merchant, carried on his business in Hamburg for the next twelve years. See Patrick Gardiner, *Schopenhauer* (Baltimore, 1963), 11.

20. Carroll, *Wallace Stevens' Supreme Fiction,* 326; Bloom, *Poems of Our Climate,* 358.

21. Carroll, *Wallace Stevens' Supreme Fiction,* 325; Gyorgyi Voros, *Notations of the Wild: Ecology in the Poetry of Wallace Stevens* (Iowa City, 1997), 67; David Michael Hertz, *Emersonian Unfoldings in Wright, Stevens, and Ives* (Carbondale, 1993), 42; Whiting, *Never-Resting Mind,* 177, 179; James Baird, *The Dome and the Rock: Structure in the Poetry of Wallace Stevens* (Baltimore, 1968), 70.

22. Voros, *Notations of the Wild,* 129.

23. Milton Bates, *Wallace Stevens: A Mythology of Self* (Berkeley, 1985), 271, 272; Hertz, *Emersonian Unfoldings in Wright, Stevens, and Ives,* 40.

24. Helen Vendler, *Wallace Stevens: Words Chosen out of Desire* (Knoxville, 1984), 44.

25. Harrison, "Not Ideas about the Thing but the Thing Itself," 667.

26. David La Guardia, *Advance on Chaos: The Sanctifying Imagination of Wallace Stevens* (Hanover, 1983), 160; Riddel, *Clairvoyant Eye,* 267; Bloom, *Poems of Our Climate,* 358; Bates, *Mythology of Self,* 272; Hertz, *Emersonian Unfoldings in Wright, Stevens, and Ives,* 40; Carroll, *Wallace Stevens' Supreme Fiction,* 327.

27. Sukenick, *Musing the Obscure,* 190.

28. Whiting, *Never-Resting Mind,* 179; Hertz, *Emersonian Unfoldings in Wright, Stevens, and Ives,* 42.

NOTES TO CHAPTER 4

1. In Randall Jarrell's 1955 review of the *Collected Poems,* for example, it is one of a handful of candidates for Stevens' greatest poem. "*The Collected Poems of Wallace Stevens,*" in *The Achievement of Wallace Stevens,* ed. Ashley Brown and Robert S. Haller (Philadelphia, 1962), 190.

2. Lea Baechler, "Pre-Elegiac Affirmation in 'To an Old Philosopher in Rome,'" *Wallace Stevens Journal* 14 (1990): 142–43.

3. Edmund Wilson, "Santayana at the Convent of the Blue Nuns," *New Yorker,* April 6, 1946, pp. 55, 61, 60.

4. Ibid., 62.

5. See Stevens, *Palm at the End of the Mind*, xiv.

6. Bloom, *Poems of Our Climate*, 361; Baechler, "Pre-Elegiac Affirmation in 'To an Old Philosopher in Rome,'" 141; Berger, *Forms of Farewell*, 140.

7. Lombardi, *Wallace Stevens and the Pennsylvania Keystone*, 245; Wilson, "Santayana at the Convent of the Blue Nuns," 59–60.

8. Discussing his teaching at Harvard in *Persons and Places*, Santayana notes that "'aesthetics' might be regarded as my specialty. Very well: although I didn't have, and haven't now, a clear notion of what 'aesthetics' may be, I undertook to give a course in that subject" (*Persons* 2:156–57). In "A General Confession" he writes, "The decorative and poetic aspects of art and nature have always fascinated me and held my attention above everything else. But in philosophy I recognize no separable thing called aesthetics" (*Philosophy* 20).

9. Harold Bloom has suggested that the voice of the first third of "Notes toward a Supreme Fiction" may have been adapted from the persona Nietzsche assumes in several texts (*Poems of Our Climate*, 177); it is as likely that the poet-ephebe relationship depicted in the opening section owes something to Stevens' sessions with Santayana.

10. Alan Perlis, *Wallace Stevens: A World of Transforming Shapes* (Lewisburg, 1976), 74; Kathleen Woodward, *At Last, The Real Distinguished Thing: The Late Poems of Eliot, Pound, Stevens, and Williams* (Columbus, 1980), 120; Beckett, *Wallace Stevens*, 194; Margaret Peterson, *Wallace Stevens and the Idealist Tradition* (Ann Arbor, 1983), 86; Baechler, "Pre-Elegiac Affirmation in 'To an Old Philosopher in Rome,'" 147; Berger, *Forms of Farewell*, 133.

11. Peterson, *Wallace Stevens and the Idealist Tradition*, 86; Berger, *Forms of Farewell*, 134, 135, 140; Voros, *Notations of the Wild*, 102, 103.

12. Edmund Wilson, "Santayana: A Boyhood between Spain and Boston," *New Yorker*, January 8, 1944, p. 56.

13. The first volume, subtitled *The Background of My Life*, was published in 1944; the second, *The Middle Span*, appeared in 1945. Santayana wished the publication of the third volume, *My Host the World*, to be delayed until after his death to avoid possible embarrassment to people he had discussed. However, he permitted the first and last chapters, "A Change of Heart" and "Epilogue: My Host the World," to be published in the *Atlantic Monthly*. They appeared in the issues of December 1948 and January 1949. *My Host the World* was published in 1953, a year after his death. See Richard C. Lyon, "Introduction," in George Santayana, *Persons and Places*, ed. William G. Holzberger and Herman J. Saatkamp Jr. (Cambridge, Mass., 1986), xxxiii.

14. Lyon, "Introduction," xxii. Santayana's definition of essences in "A General Confession" is this: "What I call essence is not something alleged to exist or subsist in some higher sphere: it is the last residuum of scepticism and analysis. Whatsoever existing fact we may think we encounter, there will be obvious features distinguishing that alleged fact from any dissimilar fact and from nothing. All such features,

discernible in sense, thought, or fancy, are essences; and the realm of essence which they compose is simply the catalogue, infinitely extensible, of all characters logically distinct and ideally possible. Apart from the events they may figure in, these essences have no existence; and since the realm of essence, by definition, is infinitely comprehensive and without bias, it can exercise no control over the existing world, nor determine what features shall occur in events, or in what order" (*Philosophy* 28–29).

15. Peterson, *Wallace Stevens and the Idealist Tradition*, 87.

16. Lyon, "Introduction," xviii–xix; Perlis, *World of Transforming Shapes*, 74; Peterson, *Wallace Stevens and the Idealist Tradition*, 87.

17. Bates, *Mythology of Self*, 211; Holly Stevens, ed., *Souvenirs and Prophecies: The Young Wallace Stevens* (New York, 1977), 68–69.

18. Joel Porte, "Introduction," in George Santayana, *Interpretations of Poetry and Religion*, ed. William G. Holzberger and Herman J. Saatkamp Jr. (Cambridge, Mass., 1989), xxix.

19. He does, however, discuss his friendship with the third member of the party that evening, Pierre la Rose (*Persons* 2:173–74).

20. The spirit for Santayana is less than a supernatural power but more than simply the poetic imagination. Richard C. Lyon puts it well: "By spirit he did not understand a mysterious or dynamic power at work in the world or in the self, but simply the scanning light of attention in man, the witness of all that passes before him. Spirit when it wakes is a child of wonder, amused, puzzled, perhaps dismayed that it should find itself in this body and amid these particular scenes. . . . Spirit, addressed to all being, is more truly itself as a traveler, participating vicariously in the lives of other persons and places. It is self-transcendent. The self is left behind in the spirit's repeated acts of imaginative projection." "Introduction," xxii–xxiii.

21. The passage states, in part, "A truly free spirit will never repent; he cannot revert to his true self, since he has no particular self to revert to. He must simply go on, as transcendental spirit actually does, from one fresh incarnation to another, in and out forever of every living thing" (*Persons* 3:2).

22. Lyon, "Introduction," xxxvi.

23. Thornton Wilder, *Our Town* (New York, 1938), 125.

NOTES TO CHAPTER 5

1. Robert Markley, "*Tristram Shandy* and 'Narrative Middles': Hillis Miller and the Style of Deconstructive Criticism," in *Rhetoric and Form: Deconstruction at Yale*, ed. Robert Con Davis and Ronald Schleifer (Norman, 1985), 181; Frank Lentricchia, *After the New Criticism* (Chicago, 1980), 162.

2. William E. Cain, "Deconstruction in America: The Recent Literary Criticism of J. Hillis Miller," *College English* 41 (1979): 379; Vincent Leitch, "The Lateral Dance:

The Deconstructive Criticism of J. Hillis Miller," *Critical Inquiry* 6 (1980): 604; Lentricchia, *After the New Criticism,* 162.

3. See, for example, Jeffrey Nealon, *Double Reading: Postmodernism after Deconstruction* (Ithaca, 1993), 22, where he argues that deconstruction "is dead in literature departments today." Although he grants that there is still a great deal of discourse being produced on deconstruction, he notes that few critics would now identify themselves as deconstructionists and the term "no longer dominates Modern Language Association conference panels." Nealon cites, among other evidence of deconstruction's demise, Barbara Johnson's 1992 address at the School of Criticism and Theory, "The Wake of Deconstruction."

4. It would be difficult to overestimate the influence of Miller's reading in Stevens criticism. It is consistently cited in commentaries on "The Rock," almost always approvingly. Bloom quotes from it extensively and refers to it as the "fullest commentary yet ventured on 'The Rock'" (*Poems of Our Climate,* 346). Anthony Whiting calls it "perhaps the single most influential deconstructive reading of Stevens" (*Never-Resting Mind,* 76), and Mary Arensberg is not alone in alluding to it as a "seminal essay" ("'Curable Separation,'" 35).

5. Harold Bloom, *Kabbalah and Criticism* (New York, 1975), 107–8.

6. J. Hillis Miller, "Theory and Practice: Response to Vincent Leitch," *Critical Inquiry* 6 (1980): 614, 611.

7. Miller, "Theory and Practice," 610.

8. The Abrams Effect was perhaps first recognized during a series of skirmishes that began with Miller's attack on the logocentric premises of M. H. Abrams' *Natural Supernaturalism.* It continued with responses by Wayne Booth and Abrams and culminated in the appearance of the three critics at a 1976 MLA session called "The Limits of Pluralism," at which Miller responded to the arguments of Booth and Abrams with "The Critic as Host." The paper, especially in its two printed versions in *Critical Inquiry* and in the book *Deconstruction and Criticism,* established deconstruction's seeming invulnerability to attack and underscored the success of Miller's rhetoric in deflecting the most rigorous critique. In Donald Pease's terms, it "makes Abrams a victim of the limitations of a less resourceful critical discourse." "J. Hillis Miller: The Other Victorian at Yale," in *The Yale Critics: Deconstruction In America,* ed. Jonathan Arac et al. (Minneapolis, 1983), 72.

9. Miller's motive for misreading is more textual or linguistic in orientation than is Bloom's oedipal motive. In "Stevens' Rock and Criticism as Cure" (*Georgia Review* 30 [1976]), Miller phrases the necessity of misreading in these terms: "The critic cannot by any means get outside the text, escape from the blind alleys of language he finds in the work. He can only rephrase them in other, *allotropic* terms" (331). More than that, "any literary text, with more or less explicitness or clarity, already reads or misreads itself" (333). In this conception the critic is merely pointing to the text's own misreading. "Sooner or later there is the encounter with an 'aporia' or impasse," which means that "deconstruction is not a dismantling of the structure of a text but a demonstration that it has already dismantled itself" (338,

341). Miller's two conceptions of misreading here appear to be at odds with one another, but both depend on assumptions about the nature of language rather than on assumptions about the relation of the poet or critic to the precursor, as in Bloom.

10. Bloom, *Poems of Our Climate,* 121.

11. J. Hillis Miller, "Deconstructing the Deconstructers," *Diacritics* 5 (1975): 24.

12. Ibid., 25.

13. Ibid., 29, 30, 31.

14. Miller, "Stevens' Rock and Criticism as Cure," 5, 10, 11; Bloom, *Poems of Our Climate,* 346.

15. The third section, which both Miller and I have largely avoided, perhaps because it seems anticlimactic, is titled "Forms of the Rock as a Night-Hymn." It is essentially an abstract definition of the rock as that which underlies all existence— "the habitation of the whole," the "starting point of the human and the end." Janet McCann notes, "The third part does in a generalized and abstract way what is done on a more personal level in part 1." *Wallace Stevens Revisited,* 126.

16. Miller, "Deconstructing the Deconstructers," 25; Miller, "Stevens' Rock and Criticism as Cure," 8, 5.

17. Miller, "Stevens' Rock and Criticism as Cure," 13.

18. Richard Hull, *The Murder of My Aunt* (New York, 1968), 241.

19. Miller, "Stevens' Rock and Criticism as Cure," 10.

20. Ibid., 20.

21. In 1953 Stevens paraphrased a passage from *The Man with the Blue Guitar* in terms that suggest why the "cure of ourselves" must be equal to the "cure of the ground": "I want, as a man of the imagination, to write poetry with all the power of a monster equal in strength to that of the monster about whom I write. I want man's imagination to be completely adequate in the face of reality" (*Letters* 790).

22. Miller, "Stevens' Rock and Criticism as Cure," 10; Miller, "Theory and Practice," 610.

23. Miller, "Stevens' Rock and Criticism as Cure," 20, 331.

24. Ibid., 331, 333, 335, 341, 343, 348.

25. In "Theory and Practice" Miller states that "unreadability" is a better term than "misreading" in referring to the heterogeneity or incoherence of texts (610). In "The Critic as Host" (*Critical Inquiry* 3 [1977]) he says of the text under discussion, "The poem, like all texts, is 'unreadable,' if by 'readable' one means open to a single, definitive, univocal interpretation" (447). In effect, then, provocative terms such as "misreading" and "unreadable" turn out to refer to a more innocuous conception, the absence of a definitive interpretation, one that would forever put an end to the interpretation, for any given text.

26. Miller, "Theory and Practice," 611.

27. Friedrich Nietzsche, *The Dawn of Day,* trans. J. M. Kennedy, vol. 9 of *The Complete Works of Friedrich Nietzsche,* ed. Oscar Levy (New York, 1964), 358; J. Hillis Miller, "*Heart of Darkness* Revisited," in Joseph Conrad, *Heart of Darkness,* ed. Ross C.

Murfin (Boston, 1996), 220; Miller, "Stevens' Rock and Criticism as Cure," 331; Miller, "Theory and Practice," 610; Markley, "*Tristram Shandy* and 'Narrative Middles,'" 182.

NOTES TO CONCLUSION

1. I am following Milton Bates' revised edition of *Opus Posthumous* for the dates of composition of these poems. Of the nineteen poems he assigns to 1954 and 1955, the dates of three—"On the Way to the Bus," "Of Mere Being," and "'A mythology reflects its region . . .'" (the transcript of which is untitled)—are conjectural. "As You Leave the Room" may have been written as late as 1955, although it is based on a shorter poem written in 1947 (*OP* vi, xi–xii, 325).

2. Alan Filreis, *Wallace Stevens and the Actual World* (Princeton, 1991), 268; Bloom, *Poems of Our Climate,* 292.

3. Filreis, *Wallace Stevens and the Actual World,* 264.

4. Ibid., 266, 265, 268.

5. Halliday, *Stevens and the Interpersonal,* 77–78.

6. Doggett, *Stevens' Poetry of Thought,* 5, 6; Beckett, *Wallace Stevens,* 205; Filreis, *Wallace Stevens and the Actual World,* 270; Randall Jarrell, "Reflections on Wallace Stevens," in *Poetry and the Age* (New York, 1972), 140.

7. Beckett, *Wallace Stevens,* 205, 206.

8. McCann, *Wallace Stevens Revisited,* 134–35.

9. Peter Brazeau, *Parts of a World: Wallace Stevens Remembered* (New York, 1983), 288.

10. Bates, *Mythology of Self,* 295.

11. Bloom, *Poems of Our Climate,* 370, 255.

12. A table of "Annual Frequency" of the aurora borealis in the eleventh edition of the *Encyclopaedia Britannica,* for example, shows that in New Haven, Connecticut, the number of auroras that occurred in summer was only slightly less than the number in fall and winter. Charles Chree, "Aurora Polaris," *Encyclopaedia Britannica,* 11th ed. (Cambridge, U.K., 1910), 2:929.

13. "The River of Rivers in Connecticut" (*CP* 533) uses the same device, the abstract and unnamed river of rivers set beside references to Farmington and Haddam.

14. Michael P. Campbell and John Dolan, "Teaching Stevens' Poetry through Rhetorical Structure," in *Teaching Wallace Stevens,* ed. John N. Serio and B. J. Leggett (Knoxville, 1994), 120; Sigmund Freud, "Negation," in *The Standard Edition of the Complete Psychological Works of Sigmund Freud,* trans. and ed. James Strachey (London, 1955), 19:235.

15. Lensing, *Wallace Stevens and the Seasons,* 128; Schwarz, *Narrative and Representation in the Poetry of Wallace Stevens,* 225.

16. See Bates in *OP,* 323.

17. Other late poems in which rooms (and a foyer) are associated with states of being are "To an Old Philosopher in Rome" (*CP* 508), "A Quiet Normal Life" (*CP* 523), "Final Soliloquy of the Interior Paramour" (*CP* 524), and "Local Objects" (*OP* 137). Lee Jenkins notes that "the poem's title is part of the motif of the threshold found in Stevens' late poetry." *Wallace Stevens: Rage for Order* (Portland, Ore., 2000), 129.

18. John Dolan, "'The warmth I had forgotten': Stevens' Revision of 'First Warmth' and the Dramatization of the Interpersonal," *Wallace Stevens Journal* 21 (1997): 162, 165; Jenkins, *Rage for Order,* 128, 129.

19. Wilder, *Our Town,* 125.

20. Lensing, *Wallace Stevens and the Seasons,* 175; Dolan, "'The warmth I had forgotten,'" 166.

21. Bloom, *Poems of Our Climate,* 370.

22. Jennifer Bates, "Stevens, Hegel, and the Palm at the End of the Mind," *Wallace Stevens Journal* 23 (1999): 152.

23. Jennifer Bates' careful reading goes back to Hegel's aesthetics to try to show why Stevens' metaphor exceeds our grasp.

24. Bloom, *Poems of Our Climate,* 370; Bates, "Stevens, Hegel, and the Palm at the End of the Mind," 125; Jarrell, "Reflections on Wallace Stevens," 137.

Abrams, M. H. "The Deconstructive Angel." *Critical Inquiry* 3 (1977): 425–38.

Adams, Richard P. "Wallace Stevens and Schopenhauer's *The World as Will and Idea.*" *Tulane Studies in English* 20 (1972): 135–68.

Arensberg, Mary. "'A Curable Separation': Stevens and the Mythology of Gender." In *Wallace Stevens and the Feminine,* edited by Melita Schaum. Tuscaloosa, 1993.

Baechler, Lea. "Pre-Elegiac Affirmation in 'To an Old Philosopher in Rome.'" *Wallace Stevens Journal* 14 (1990): 141–52.

Baird, James. *The Dome and the Rock: Structure in the Poetry of Wallace Stevens.* Baltimore, 1968.

Bates, Jennifer. "Stevens, Hegel, and the Palm at the End of the Mind." *Wallace Stevens Journal* 23 (1999): 152–66.

Bates, Milton. *Wallace Stevens: A Mythology of Self.* Berkeley, 1985.

Beckett, Lucy. *Wallace Stevens.* London, 1974.

Berger, Charles. *Forms of Farewell: The Late Poetry of Wallace Stevens.* Madison, 1985.

Blessing, Richard. *Wallace Stevens' "Whole Harmonium."* Syracuse, 1970.

Bloom, Harold. *Kabbalah and Criticism.* New York, 1975.

———. *Wallace Stevens: The Poems of Our Climate.* Ithaca, 1977.

Booth, Wayne C. "'Preserving the Exemplar': or, How Not to Dig Our Own Graves." *Critical Inquiry* 3 (1977): 407–23.

Brazeau, Peter. *Parts of a World: Wallace Stevens Remembered.* New York, 1983.

Brogan, Jacqueline Vaught. "'Sisters of the Minotaur': Sexism and Stevens." In *Wallace Stevens and the Feminine,* edited by Melita Schaum. Tuscaloosa, 1993.

Burney, William. *Wallace Stevens.* New York, 1968.

Cain, William E. "Deconstruction in America: The Recent Literary Criticism of J. Hillis Miller." *College English* 41 (1979): 367–82.

Campbell, P. Michael, and John Dolan. "Teaching Stevens' Poetry through Rhetorical Structure." In *Teaching Wallace Stevens,* edited by John N. Serio and B. J. Leggett. Knoxville, 1994.

Carroll, Joseph. *Wallace Stevens' Supreme Fiction: A New Romanticism.* Baton Rouge, 1987.

Chree, Charles. "Aurora Polaris." *Encyclopaedia Britannica.* Vol. 2. 11th ed. Cambridge, U.K., 1910.

Cook, Eleanor. *Poetry, Word-Play, and Word-War in Wallace Stevens.* Princeton, 1988.

Davis, William V. "'This Refuge That the End Creates': Stevens' 'Not Ideas about the Thing but the Thing Itself.'" *Wallace Stevens Journal* 11 (1987): 103–10.

Doggett, Frank. *Stevens' Poetry of Thought.* Baltimore, 1966.

Dolan, John. "'The warmth I had forgotten': Stevens' Revision of 'First Warmth' and the Dramatization of the Interpersonal." *Wallace Stevens Journal* 21 (1997): 162–74.

Donoghue, Denis. *Connoisseurs of Chaos: Ideas of Order in Modern American Poetry.* 2nd ed. New York, 1984.

Emerson, Dorothy. "Wallace Stevens' Sky That Thinks." *Wallace Stevens Journal* 9 (1985): 71–84.

Filreis, Alan. *Wallace Stevens and the Actual World.* Princeton, 1991.

Fisher, Barbara. *Wallace Stevens: The Intensest Rendezvous.* Charlottesville, 1990.

———. "A Woman with the Hair of a Pythoness." In *Wallace Stevens and the Feminine,* edited by Melita Schaum. Tuscaloosa, 1993.

Freud, Sigmund. "Negation." In *The Standard Edition of the Complete Psychological Works of Sigmund Freud,* translated and edited by James Strachey. Vol. 19. London, 1955.

Gardiner, Patrick. *Schopenhauer.* Baltimore, 1963.

Grey, Thomas C. *The Wallace Stevens Case: Law and the Practice of Poetry.* Cambridge, Mass., 1991.

Halliday, Mark. *Stevens and the Interpersonal.* Princeton, 1991.

Harrison, Robert Pogue. "'Not Ideas about the Thing but the Thing Itself.'" *New Literary History* 30 (1999): 661–73.

Hertz, David Michael. *Emersonian Unfoldings in Wright, Stevens, and Ives.* Carbondale, 1993.

Hobbs, Michael. "Stevens' Gunman Lover: Readers in *The Rock.*" *Wallace Stevens Journal* 18 (1994): 157–69.

Hull, Richard. *The Murder of My Aunt.* New York, 1968.

Humphries, David. "A New Kind of Meditation: Wallace Stevens' 'The Plain Sense of Things.'" *Wallace Stevens Journal* 23 (1999): 27–47.

Jarraway, David R. *Wallace Stevens and the Question of Belief: Metaphysician in the Dark.* Baton Rouge, 1993.

Jarrell, Randall. "*The Collected Poems of Wallace Stevens.*" In *The Achievement of Wallace Stevens,* edited by Ashley Brown and Robert S. Haller. Philadelphia, 1962.

———. "Randall Jarrell Discovers 'a Great Poem of a New Kind.'" In *Wallace Stevens: The Critical Heritage,* edited by Charles Doyle. London, 1985.

———. "Reflections on Wallace Stevens." In *Poetry and the Age.* New York, 1972.

Jenkins, Lee M. *Wallace Stevens: Rage for Order.* Portland, Ore., 2000.

Johnson, Barbara. "*Les Fleurs du mal armé:* Some Reflections on Intertextuality." In *Lyric Poetry: Beyond the New Criticism,* edited by Chaviva Hosek and Patricia Parker. Ithaca, 1985.

Kessler, Edward. *Images of Wallace Stevens.* New Brunswick, 1972.

La Guardia, David M. *Advance on Chaos: The Sanctifying Imagination of Wallace Stevens.* Hanover, 1983.

Leggett, B. J. *Wallace Stevens and Poetic Theory: Conceiving the Supreme Fiction.* Chapel Hill, 1987.

Leitch, Vincent. "The Lateral Dance: The Deconstructive Criticism of J. Hillis Miller." *Critical Inquiry* 6 (1980): 593–607.

Lensing, George. *Wallace Stevens: A Poet's Growth.* Baton Rouge, 1986.

———. *Wallace Stevens and the Seasons.* Baton Rouge, 2001.

Lentricchia, Frank. *After the New Criticism.* Chicago, 1980.

———. *Modernist Quartet.* Cambridge, U.K., 1994.

Lombardi, Thomas Francis. *Wallace Stevens and the Pennsylvania Keystone: The Influence of Origins on His Life and Poetry.* Selinsgrove, 1996.

Lowell, Robert. "For George Santayana." *Life Studies.* New York, 1959.

Lyon, Richard C. "Introduction." In George Santayana, *Persons and Places.* edited by William G. Holzberger and Herman J. Saatkamp Jr. Cambridge, Mass., 1986.

Markley, Robert. "*Tristram Shandy* and 'Narrative Middles': Hillis Miller and the Style of Deconstructive Criticism." In *Rhetoric and Form: Deconstruction at Yale,* edited by Robert Con Davis and Ronald Schleifer. Norman, 1985.

McCann, Janet. *Wallace Stevens Revisited: "The Celestial Possible."* New York, 1995.

Miller, J. Hillis. "The Critic as Host." *Critical Inquiry* 3 (1977): 439–47.

———. "Deconstructing the Deconstructers." *Diacritics* 5 (1975): 24–31.

———. "*Heart of Darkness* Revisited." In Joseph Conrad, *Heart of Darkness: Complete, Authoritative Text with Bibliographical and Historical Contexts, Critical History, and Essays from Five Contemporary Critical Perspectives,* edited by Ross C. Murfin. Boston, 1996.

———. "Stevens' Rock and Criticism as Cure." *Georgia Review* 30 (1976): 5–31, 330–48.

———. "Theory and Practice: Response to Vincent Leitch." *Critical Inquiry* 6 (1980): 609–14.

Morris, Adalaide Kirby. *Wallace Stevens: Imagination and Faith.* Princeton, 1974.

Moynihan, Robert. "Checklist: Second Purchase, Wallace Stevens Collection, Huntington Library." *Wallace Stevens Journal* 20 (1996): 76–103.

Nealon, Jeffrey. *Double Reading: Postmodernism after Deconstruction.* Ithaca, 1993.

Nietzsche, Friedrich. *The Dawn of Day,* translated by J. M. Kennedy. Vol. 9 of *The Complete Works of Friedrich Nietzsche,* edited by Oscar Levy. New York, 1964.

Patke, Rajeev S. *The Long Poems of Wallace Stevens: An Interpretative Study.* Cambridge, U.K., 1985.

Pease, Donald. "J. Hillis Miller: The Other Victorian at Yale." In *The Yale Critics: Deconstruction in America,* edited by Jonathan Arac et al. Minneapolis, 1983.

Perlis, Alan. *Wallace Stevens: A World of Transforming Shapes.* Lewisburg, 1976.

Peterson, Margaret. *Wallace Stevens and the Idealist Tradition.* Ann Arbor, 1983.

Porte, Joel. "Introduction." In George Santayana, *Interpretations of Poetry and Religion,* edited by William G. Holzberger and Herman J. Saatkamp Jr. Cambridge, Mass., 1989.

Regueiro, Helen. *The Limits of Imagination: Wordsworth, Yeats, and Stevens.* Ithaca, 1976.

Rehder, Robert. *The Poetry of Wallace Stevens.* London, 1988.

Riddel, Joseph. *The Clairvoyant Eye: The Poetry and Poetics of Wallace Stevens.* Baton Rouge, 1965.

Riffaterre, Michael. *Semiotics of Poetry.* Bloomington, 1978.

Rogers, Arthur Kenyon. *A Student's History of Philosophy.* 3rd ed. New York, 1932.

Rusk, Loren. "Penelope's Creative Desiring: 'The World as Meditation.'" *Wallace Stevens Journal* 9 (1985): 15–25.

Santayana, George. *Apologia Pro Mente Sua.* In *The Philosophy of George Santayana,* edited by Paul Arthur Schilpp. Evanston, 1940.

———. "A General Confession." In *The Philosophy of George Santayana,* edited by Paul Arthur Schilpp. Evanston, 1940.

———. *Interpretations of Poetry and Religion,* edited by William G. Holzberger and Herman J. Saatkamp Jr. Cambridge, Mass., 1989.

———. *Persons and Places.* Vol. 1, *The Background of My Life.* New York, 1944.

———. *Persons and Places.* Vol. 2, *The Middle Span.* New York, 1945.

———. *Persons and Places.* Vol. 3, *My Host the World.* New York, 1953.

Schopenhauer, Arthur. *The Wisdom of Life: Being the First Part of Arthur Schopenhauer's Aphorismen zur Lebensweisheit,* translated by T. Bailey Saunders. London, 1924.

———. *Counsels and Maxims: Being the Second Part of Arthur Schopenhauer's Aphorismen zur Lebensweisheit,* translated by T. Bailey Saunders. London, 1924.

———. *The World as Will and Idea,* translated by R. B. Haldane and J. Kemp. 3 vols. London, 1883.

Schwarz, Daniel R. *Narrative and Representation in the Poetry of Wallace Stevens.* New York, 1993.

Stevens, Holly, ed. *Letters of Wallace Stevens.* New York, 1977.

———, ed. *The Palm at the End of the Mind.* New York, 1972.

———, ed. *Souvenirs and Prophecies: The Young Wallace Stevens.* New York, 1977.

Stevens, Wallace. *The Collected Poems of Wallace Stevens.* New York, 1954.

———. *The Necessary Angel: Essays on Reality and Imagination.* New York, 1951.

———. *Opus Posthumous,* edited by Milton J. Bates. New York, 1989.

Sukenick, Ronald. *Wallace Stevens: Musing the Obscure.* New York, 1967.

Tindall, William York. *Wallace Stevens.* Minneapolis, 1961.

Vendler, Helen. *On Extended Wings: Wallace Stevens' Longer Poems.* Cambridge, Mass., 1969.

———. *Wallace Stevens: Words Chosen out of Desire.* Knoxville, 1984.

Voros, Gyorgyi. *Notations of the Wild: Ecology in the Poetry of Wallace Stevens.* Iowa City, 1997.

Wagner, C. Roland. "Wallace Stevens: The Concealed Self." In *Wallace Stevens and the Feminine*, edited by Melita Schaum. Tuscaloosa, 1993.

Whiting, Anthony. *The Never-Resting Mind: Wallace Stevens' Romantic Irony*. Ann Arbor, 1996.

Wilder, Thornton. *Our Town*. New York, 1938.

Wilson, Edmund. "Santayana: A Boyhood between Spain and Boston." *New Yorker*, January 8, 1944, pp. 56–58.

———. "Santayana at the Convent of the Blue Nuns." *New Yorker*, April 6, 1946, pp. 55–62.

Woodward, Kathleen. *At Last, The Real Distinguished Thing: The Late Poems of Eliot, Pound, Stevens, and Williams*. Columbus, Ohio, 1980.

Abrams, M. H., 94, 152*n*8
Abrams Effect, 96, 152*n*8
"Adagia" (Stevens), 1, 49, 105, 106, 111
Adams, Henry, 80
Adams, Richard P., 35–36, 147*n*9
"Angel Surrounded by Paysans"
    (Stevens), 146*n*15
Apologia Pro Mente Sua (Santayana),
    82–83, 85–86
"The Apparitions" (Yeats), 139
Arensberg, Mary, 52, 53, 55, 59
"Artificial Populations" (Stevens), 15,
    131–33
"As You Leave the Room" (Stevens),
    113, 133–39, 154*n*1
"Asides on the Oboe" (Stevens), 5
Aurora borealis, 127, 129, 154*n*12
The Auroras of Autumn (Stevens), ix, 4,
    6, 10–15, 113
"The Auroras of Autumn" (Stevens), 1,
    4, 10–13, 17, 18, 102, 127–29, 146*n*12,
    146*n*15

The Background of My Life (San-
    tayana), 150*n*13
Baechler, Lea, 73–75, 76, 79
Baird, James, 65
Bates, Jennifer, 140, 141, 155*n*23
Bates, Milton, 66–67, 70, 86, 127
Baudelaire, Charles-Pierre, 14
Beckett, Lucy, 47, 58, 79, 123, 124
Bennett, Joseph, 47, 48
Berger, Charles, xi, 28, 55, 76, 79, 80

Blessing, Richard, 48, 59
Bloom, Harold: on "Final Soliloquy of
    the Interior Paramour," x, 51–52, 55;
    on misreading, x, xi, 93, 97, 98,
    152–53*n*9; on Stevens' last phase, x;
    on "Credences of Summer," 8; on
    "The World as Meditation," 58, 59;
    on "Looking across the Fields and
    Watching the Birds Fly," 65, 70; on
    "To an Old Philosopher in Rome,"
    76; Miller on criticism of, 93, 110;
    on meaning, 95; on "Mr. Burnshaw
    and the Statue," 97; on Miller's
    reading of "The Rock," 100, 152*n*4;
    on "The Owl in the Sarcophagus,"
    115; on aurora borealis, 127; on
    "Auroras of Autumn," 127; on "Of
    Mere Being," 139; on "A mythology
    reflects its region . . . ," 143; on
    "Notes toward a Supreme Fiction,"
    150*n*9
Booth, Wayne, 152*n*8
Brogan, Jacqueline, 52
Burney, William, 29, 59

Cain, William E., 94
Campbell, P. Michael, 129–30, 131
Carroll, Joseph, 4, 13–14, 52, 64, 65, 70
"A Change of Heart" (Santayana),
    89–91
"A Child Asleep in Its Own Life"
    (Stevens), 114, 125–27
Church, Barbara, 87

Church, Henry, 2
"Church Going" (Larkin), 67
"The Circus Animals' Desertion"
    (Yeats), 133
"A Clear Day and No Memories"
    (Stevens), 15, 129–31, 132, 133, 140, 142
"A Collect of Philosophy" (Stevens),
    36, 37–38, 47, 72
Collected Poems (Stevens), ix, 20, 22,
    113, 149n1
Columbia University, 113–18, 120–23
Conrad, Joseph, 111
Cook, Eleanor, 23
Counsels and Maxims (Schopenhauer),
    30, 40–41
"The Course of a Particular" (Stevens),
    140, 142
"Credences of Summer" (Stevens),
    6–9, 10, 11, 133, 138
"The Critic as Host" (Miller), 100,
    152n8

Davis, William V., 36
The Dawn of Day (Nietzsche), 111
De Man, Paul, 93, 94, 110
"Deconstructing the Deconstructers"
    (Miller), 93, 97–99
Deconstruction, x, 93–99, 109–12,
    152n3, 152nn8–9
Derrida, Jacques, 93, 94, 95, 98, 99, 110
"Description without Place" (Stevens),
    114
Deutsch, Babette, 114, 115, 123
Doggett, Frank, 28, 58, 62, 123
Dolan, John, 129–30, 131, 135–37, 138
Donoghue, Denis, 48–49

"Effects of Analogy" (Stevens), 22
Eliot, T. S., 14
Emerson, Dorothy, 145n9
Emerson, Ralph Waldo, 64–66, 70, 87
"The Emperor of Ice-Cream," 126
Enesco, Georges, 15, 56–57

Essence and existence, 82–83, 85–86,
    150–51n14
"Examination of the Hero in a Time
    of War" (Stevens), 138

Filreis, Alan, 114–17, 120, 121, 123–24
"Final Soliloquy of the Interior Para-
    mour" (Stevens): critics on, x,
    48–49, 51–53, 55, 148n8; and
    supreme fiction, 4, 48; on God and
    imagination, 6, 47, 48–52, 54–56,
    102; parallel worlds in, 24–25; com-
    pared with other poems by
    Stevens, 26–27, 39, 50, 54, 56, 57, 59,
    62, 63, 72, 91, 118, 140; on poverty,
    42, 91; as fragment of projected
    long poem, 47, 48; significance of,
    for Stevens, 47–48; placement of,
    in The Rock, 48; publication of, 48,
    148n10; beginning of, 49–50; candle
    metaphor in, 51; identity of
    "interior paramour" in, 52–55;
    meaning of term paramour, 53;
    interiority and exteriority in,
    54–55; meaning of term final in,
    55–56; independent reality in, 140;
    room associated with states of
    being in, 155n17
"First Warmth" (Stevens), 133–37, 138
Fisher, Barbara, 52, 53, 60, 63
"For George Santayana" (Lowell), 73, 77
Freud, Sigmund, 130

"A General Confession" (Santayana),
    85, 150n8, 150–51n14
Georgia Review, 93
"The Green Plant" (Stevens), 28, 43–45
Grey, Thomas, 53

Halliday, Mark, 59, 119
Harrison, Robert Pogue, 25, 69
Hartman, Geoffrey, 93, 94, 110
Harvard University, 78, 80, 82, 86–87, 114

Heart of Darkness (Conrad), 111
Hegel, G. W. F., 155n23
Heidegger, Martin, 98, 99
Hertz, David Michael, 65, 66, 70, 71
Hobbs, Michael, 146n2
Homer, 117
Hudson Review, 47, 51, 75, 148n10
Hull, Richard, 105
Humphries, David, 146nn12–13

"The Idea of Order at Key West"
    (Stevens), 68
Ideas of Order (Stevens), 134
Imagination: and imagination-reality
    theme, 1, 5–7, 9–10, 12–13; and God,
    5–6, 47, 48–52, 54–56; and supreme
    reality, 5–7, 9–10, 12–13; reality as
    independent of poet's imagination,
    6–10, 12–13; in "The Auroras of
    Autumn," 10–13, 17, 18, 102, 127–29,
    146n12, 146n15; in "The Plain Sense
    of Things," 10, 17–19, 57, 102, 141,
    146nn12–13; and "essential poem"
    or "central poem," 14; in "The
    Rock," 18, 102; in "An Ordinary
    Evening in New Haven," 19–20;
    and "Not Ideas about the Thing
    but the Thing Itself," 20–22; can-
    dles as image of, 27; in "A Quiet
    Normal Life," 27–28; in "Final
    Soliloquy of the Interior Para-
    mour," 47, 48–52, 54–56; in "The
    World as Meditation," 60–61, 63,
    102; and Santayana, 77–78, 87,
    88–89; value of, in life, 77–78; and
    cure of ourselves, 108; Stevens on,
    from "The Man with the Blue Gui-
    tar," 153n21
"Imagination as Value" (Stevens), 73,
    77, 78, 89
Interpretations of Poetry and Religion
    (Santayana), 80, 86–87
Intertextuality, xi, 20–21

The Inverted Bell (Riddel), 94, 97–99
"The Irish Cliffs of Moher" (Stevens),
    134

Jarraway, David, 3, 8
Jarrell, Randall, 58, 123–24, 143, 149n1
Jenkins, Lee, 137, 155n17
Johnson, Barbara, 20, 152n3

Kessler, Edward, 28, 48

La Guardia, David, 70
La Rose, Pierre, 86–87, 151n19
"Large Red Man Reading" (Stevens), 13
Larkin, Philip, 67
"Lebensweisheitspielerei" (Stevens),
    28–30, 38–42, 43, 91
Leitch, Vincent, 94, 95–96
Lensing, George, 56–61, 130, 138
Lentricchia, Frank, 59, 60, 94
"Life on a Battleship" (Stevens), 55
Liminality, 81, 137–38, 155n17
"Local Objects" (Stevens), 131, 155n17
Lombardi, Thomas, 28, 29, 73, 76
"Long and Sluggish Lines" (Stevens),
    15, 103
"Looking across the Fields and Watch-
    ing the Birds Fly" (Stevens): and
    supreme fiction, 12, 15, 17; parallel
    worlds in, 24; on God and imagi-
    nation, 47, 102; compared with
    other poems by Stevens, 56, 63, 67,
    68, 72, 75; publication of, 56, 63, 75;
    Mr. Homburg in, 63–67, 69, 70–71,
    75; tone of, 63–64, 66–67; critics
    on, 64–66, 70, 71; "pensive nature"
    in, 64–69, 146n15; and Schopen-
    hauer, 64, 69–70, 72; and transcen-
    dental thought, 64–66; identity of
    new scholar and older scholar in,
    70–71; nature versus human mind
    in, 71–72
Lowell, Robert, 73, 77

Lucifer (Santayana), 86
Lyon, Richard C., 82, 83, 89–90, 151*n*20

"Man and Bottle" (Stevens), 105
"The Man with the Blue Guitar"
    (Stevens), 147*n*9, 153*n*21
Markley, Robert, 93–94, 112
McCann, Janet, 3–4, 49, 73, 123, 124–25,
    153*n*15
McCarthy, Joseph, 116
Meaning versus significance, x–xi
The Middle Span (Santayana), 150n13
Miller, J. Hillis: and deconstruction, x,
    93–99, 109–12, 152*nn*8–9; on mis-
    reading, x, xi, 93, 95, 96, 97–98,
    110–12, 152–53*n*9; on "The Rock," x,
    93–97, 100–112, 146*n*17, 152*n*4;
    "Deconstructing the Deconstruc-
    ters" by, 93, 97–99; on Riddel, 94,
    97–99; "Stevens' Rock and Criti-
    cism as Cure" by, 94, 100–104,
    109–12; "The Critic as Host" by,
    100, 152*n*8; on unreadability, 103,
    107, 111, 112, 153*n*25; on criticism as
    cure of the ground, 109–10; on
    Heart of Darkness, 111
Misreading: in poststructuralist criti-
    cism, ix–x; Bloom on, x, xi, 93, 97,
    98, 152–53*n*9; Miller on, x, xi, 93, 95,
    97–99, 110–12, 152–53*n*9; strong ver-
    sus weak misreadings, x, 93, 96–99,
    103; by Riddel, 94, 97–99; and
    deconstruction, 97–99, 110–12,
    152*n*9; motives for, 152–53*n*9
"Le Monocle de Mon Oncle"
    (Stevens), 67
Morris, Adalaide Kirby, 52
"Mr. Burnshaw and the Statue"
    (Stevens), 97
The Murder of My Aunt (Hull), 105
My Host the World (Santayana), 150n13
"A mythology reflects its region . . ."
    (Stevens), 142–43, 154*n*1

The Nation, 28, 87
Nealon, Jeffrey, 152*n*3
The Necessary Angel (Stevens), 1
"Negation" (Freud), 130
The New Yorker, 73, 77, 80, 85
Nietzsche, Friedrich, xi, 30, 94, 111,
    150*n*9
"Not Ideas about the Thing but the
    Thing Itself" (Stevens), 20–22,
    25–27, 35–38, 61, 69, 140
"Note on Moonlight" (Stevens), 16–17
"Notes toward a Supreme Fiction"
    (Stevens): and supreme fiction,
    1–3, 9; critics on, 2–3, 150*n*9; com-
    pared with other poems by
    Stevens, 6, 62; and Schopenhauer's
    ideas, 33–34, 147*n*9; "final good" in,
    55; relationship between poet and
    ephebe in, 78; and Santayana's
    ideas, 86
"Nuns Painting Water-Lilies"
    (Stevens), 15

"Of Mere Being" (Stevens), 113, 139–42,
    154*n*1
"Of Modern Poetry" (Stevens), 105–6
"An Old Man Asleep" (Stevens), 22–24,
    28, 75, 146*n*2
"On the Way to the Bus" (Stevens),
    154*n*1
"One of the Inhabitants of the West"
    (Stevens), 15
Opus Posthumous (Stevens), ix, 15,
    154*n*1. *See also* specific poems
"An Ordinary Evening in New Haven"
    (Stevens), 6, 13, 19–20, 63, 147*n*9
Our Town (Wilder), 91, 137
"The Owl in the Sarcophagus"
    (Stevens), 4, 13–14, 79, 115
"Owl's Clover" (Stevens), 5

Parts of a World (Stevens), ix
Patke, Rafeev, 2–3

Pease, Donald, 152*n*8

Penelope, 57–63, 67, 68, 75, 118, 119

Perlis, Alan, 79, 83

Persons and Places (Santayana), 80–83, 85, 87–91, 150*n*8

"Peter Quince at the Clavier" (Stevens), 67

Peterson, Margaret, 79, 83, 86

"The Plain Sense of Things" (Stevens): critics on, 4, 146*nn*12–13; and supreme fiction, 4, 15–19, 102; and imagination, 10, 17–19, 57, 102, 141, 146*nn*12–13; publication of, 28, 43; and facts of ordinary life, 30; compared with other poems by Stevens, 39, 40–41, 44

"The Planet on the Table" (Stevens), 44, 45–46

Porte, Joel, 87

Poststructuralism, ix–x, 94

Praeteritic antithesis, 129–30, 131

"Presence of an External Master of Knowledge" (Stevens), 15, 114, 118–21, 127

"A Primitive Like an Orb" (Stevens), 4, 13–14

"Puella Parvula" (Stevens), 13

"A Quiet Normal Life" (Stevens), 15, 26–28, 30, 39, 50, 54, 155*n*17

"Reality Is an Activity of the Most August Imagination" (Stevens), 15, 127

"The Region November" (Stevens), 140, 142

Regueiro, Helen, 43–45

Rehder, Robert, 2

"The Relations between Poetry and Painting" (Stevens), 14

Riddel, Joseph, 2, 8, 70, 94, 97–99

Riffaterre, Michael, x–xi

"The River of Rivers in Connecticut" (Stevens), 23, 154*n*13

"The Rock" (Stevens): Miller's reading of, x, 93–97, 100–112, 146*n*17, 152*n*4; master intertext of, 3; Carroll on, 4; and supreme fiction, 4, 15; and imagination, 18, 102; parallel worlds in, 24; and deconstructive criticism, 93–94, 109–10; "cure of the ground" in, 100–101, 103, 105–11; first section of ("Seventy Years Later"), 101–4, 107; nothingness or meaninglessness in, 101–4, 108; external consciousness in, 102, 132; "gross universe" in, 103–4; Miller on unreadability of, 103, 107, 111, 112; second section ("Poem as Icon") of, 103–8; "cure of ourselves" in, 104–8; critics on, 153*n*15; third section of, 153*n*15

The Rock (Stevens): personal and accessible nature of, ix, 113; and supreme fiction, 2, 4–5, 15–22; Carroll on, 4; imagination in, 12, 15, 50, 55; last poem of, 20–22; opening poem of, 22–24; parallel worlds in, 22–29, 31, 46, 75; seasonal motif in, 22; ambiguity of reference in, 23; and Schopenhauer's ideas, 29–46; facts of ordinary life in, 30; on cycles of desire and ennui, 33–34; voice of old age and poverty in, 39–42, 43–46, 53, 75–76, 79, 91; on reality, 44; thematic core of, 72; on clarity of vision through renunciation and destitution, 90, 118; and Santayana's ideas, 91–92; compared with "The Sail of Ulysses," 118; on knowledge and being, 118, 123; rooms and houses in, 134, 155*n*17; winter landscape in, 136. *See also* specific poems

Rogers, Arthur Kenyon, 36

Royce, Josiah, 82

Rusk, Loren, 59, 62

"The Sail of Ulysses" (Stevens): as Phi Beta Kappa poem at Columbia, 113–18, 120–23; Stevens' disappointment with, 113–14, 123; and "A Child Asleep in Its Own Life," 114, 125–27; and "Presence of an External Master of Knowledge," 114, 118–21, 127; Filreis on, 115–17, 120, 121, 123–24; on knowledge and being, 115–20; on right to knowledge, 115–18, 120–23; and "The World as Meditation," 115, 118, 119; Ulysses in, 116–22, 124–25; on loneliness and knowledge, 118–19; parallel lives and knowledges in, 120–21; great Omnium in, 121, 122; on poverty and transcendence, 121–22; sibyl in, 121–22, 125; critics on, 123–25; style of, 123–24

"Sailing to Byzantium" (Yeats), 143

Santayana, George: and Stevens' late poetry generally, xi; portrait of, in "To an Old Philosopher in Rome," 24, 46, 73–92, 137–38, 139; in Roman convent, 73–77, 85, 90, 91; Wilson's portrait of, in The New Yorker, 73–77, 85; and religion, 76–77, 80, 86, 87–88; as aesthetician, 77–78, 150n8; at Harvard, 78, 82, 86–87; Stevens' relationship with, 78, 86–87; memoir by, 80–83, 85, 87–91, 150n13; on Rome, 81, 88; on existence and essence, 82–83, 85–86, 150–51n14; on spirit, 82, 88–89, 151nn20–21; and "Notes toward a Supreme Fiction," 86; on imagination, 87, 88–89; and transcendentalism, 87; on old age, 88–89; personal crisis or metanoia of, 90; teaching career of, 150n8. See also specific works

Saunders, T. Bailey, 29–31, 36–37, 40

Schopenhauer, Arthur: and Stevens' late poetry generally, xi, 29–46; and "Lebensweisheitspielerei," 29–30, 38–41; and The Rock, 29–32; on happiness, 30–31, 42; and two worlds of will and idea, 31–32; on will, 32–33, 35, 36–37, 42, 46, 69; on cycles of desire and ennui, 33, 34; on heaven, 33; on suffering, 33, 42–43; on thing-in-itself, 35–37; on morning dream versus reality, 36; on nature, 36; summary of theory of, 37–38; on old age, 40–43, 45; on fame, 43; and "Looking across the Fields and Watching the Birds Fly," 64, 69–70, 72; youth of, in Hamburg, 149n19. See also specific works

Schwarz, Daniel, 2, 130–31

Selected Poems (Stevens), 48

Sewanee Review, 131, 132

Shelley, Percy Bysshe, 97

Significance versus meaning, x–xi

Simons, Hi, 2, 5

"The Snow Man" (Stevens), 6, 28, 147n9

"Solitaire under the Oaks" (Stevens), 129, 131

"Someone Puts a Pineapple Together" (Stevens), 138

Spirit, 82, 88–89, 151nn20–21. See also Imagination

Stevens, Holly, 114, 126, 139

Stevens, Peter, 126

Stevens, Wallace: and Schopenhauer's ideas, xi, 29–46; imagination-reality theme of, 1, 5–7, 9–10, 12–13; and supreme fiction, 1–4; on God/gods, 5–6, 47; on imagination, 6; reading by, 30, 35, 80, 86; on cycles of desire and ennui, 33–34; epigraphs for poems by, 56–57, 67; marriage of, 59, 60; beginnings of poems by, 67; conversion of, 76;

death of, 76; at Harvard, 78, 80, 86–87; Santayana's relationship with, 78, 86–87; on old age, 113; as Phi Beta Kappa poet, 113–15; style of late poems by, 123–24; titles of poems by, 127; early poetry by, 145*n*9. *See also* specific poems, books of poetry, and other writings
"Stevens' Rock and Criticism as Cure" (Miller), 94, 100–104, 109–12
"Study of Images II" (Stevens), 64
Sukenick, Ronald, 48, 71
"The Sun This March" (Stevens), 134
"Sunday Morning" (Stevens), 11, 33, 66
Supreme fiction: Stevens on, 1–2; critics on, 2–4; and *The Rock,* 2, 4–5, 15–22, 102; in Stevens' late poetry generally, 3–4; and "Final Soliloquy of the Interior Paramour," 4, 48, 102; and God/gods, 5–6, 47; and imagination, 5–10, 12–13; and *The Auroras of Autumn,* 10–15; and "The Plain Sense of Things," 15–19, 102; and intertextuality, 20–21; and "Not Ideas about the Thing but the Thing Itself," 20–22

Taylor, Horace, 114, 115, 118, 121
"Tea at the Palaz of Hoon" (Stevens), 147*n*9
Tennyson, Alfred Lord, 117
"Theory and Practice: Response to Vincent Leitch" (Miller), 95–96
"Things of August" (Stevens), 13
Thomas, Dylan, 11, 45
"Three Academic Pieces" (Stevens), 138
Threshold, 81, 137–38, 155*n*7
Times Literary Supplement, 114, 125
Tindall, William York, 2
"To an Old Philosopher in Rome" (Stevens): difficulties in reading, ix, 93; and supreme fiction, 4; San-

tayana's vision in, 8, 78–82, 84–85, 89; parallel worlds in, 24, 75, 82, 83, 85; as portrait of Santayana, 24, 46, 73–92, 137–38, 139; on poverty and old age, 41–42, 75–76, 79, 81, 91; and Wilson's portrait of Santayana, 73–77, 85; compared with other poems by Stevens, 75, 91, 137–38; publication of, 75, 148*n*10; critics on, 76, 79–80, 83; afterlife in, 79–80; and Santayana's writings as intertexts, 80–83, 85–91; and liminality, 81, 82, 137–38; spatial metaphor in, 83–84; on clarity of vision through renunciation, 90–91; room associated with state of being in, 155*n*7
Tomlinson, Charles, 6
"Tradition and the Individual Talent" (Eliot), 14
Transcendentalism, 64–66, 87
Transport to Summer (Stevens), ix, 6, 133
"Two or Three Ideas" (Stevens), 5–6

"The Ultimate Poem Is Abstract" (Stevens), 13, 63–64
Ulysses: in "The World as Meditation," 57–63, 67, 68, 75, 148*n*14; in "The Sail of Ulysses," 116–22, 124–25; of Homer, 117; of Tennyson, 117; in "Presence of an External Master of Knowledge," 119–20
Unreadability, 103, 107, 111, 112, 153*n*25

"Vacancy in the Park" (Stevens), 131
Vendler, Helen, 8, 10, 67
Voros, Gyorgyi, 65, 66, 80

Wagner, C. Roland, 63
Weinstock, Herbert, 48, 133
"The Well Dressed Man with a Beard" (Stevens), 138

Whiting, Anthony, 18, 48, 65, 71, 152*n*4
Wilder, Thornton, 91, 137
Will, Schopenhauer on, 32–33, 35, 36–37, 42, 46, 69
Williams, William Carlos, 97, 98, 99
Wilson, Edmund, 73–77, 80, 85
The Wisdom of Life (Schopenhauer), 29–32, 36–37, 43
Woodward, Kathleen, 79
"The World as Meditation" (Stevens): and supreme fiction, 15, 17; parallel worlds in, 24; imagination in, 47, 60–61, 63, 102; compared with other poems by Stevens, 56, 57, 59, 61, 62, 63, 67, 68, 69, 72, 75, 115, 118, 119; epigraph of, 56–57, 60; publication of, 56, 75; ambiguity of, 57–58; Penelope and Ulysses in, 57–63, 67, 68, 75, 118, 119; critics on, 58–60, 62–63; sun-Ulysses parallels in, 58, 61–62
The World as Will and Idea (Schopenhauer), 30–36, 42–43, 46, 69

Yale School of criticism, 93
Yeats, W. B., 80, 133, 134, 136, 139, 143